BLINDSIDED BY MOTHER HOOD

Dr. Davies,

You've been an amazing support for Jesse over the last eight years! Thank you for always listening so well, and for having an open mind. We appreciate you very much!!

Pre Baby, New Baby, Big Baby

Blindsided by Motherhood

An Uncensored Glimpse
for the Unseasoned Mom

By Nicole Ampi

GreenTree Publishers
Newnan, Georgia

Published in Newnan, Georgia by Green Tree Publishers.
For information and for other Green Tree titles visit
www.greentreepublishers.com

ISBN: 978-1-944483-23-4

Heather Griffin-Vine I Vine Design

Dedication

I dedicate this book to my daughters, Ryanne and Reese, who will someday, God willing, become mothers facing their own challenges of motherhood. Motherhood is the best gift that God can give, but it requires understanding and realistic expectations. I hope this book will serve as a useful guide when you begin your motherhood journey.
I love you.

Table of Contents

Acknowledgments

When I finished this book, I had been writing for over ten years. The hours away from my kids and husband were numerous. I never imagined I would end up with something as detailed and polished as this book.

There is no one who deserves appreciation and acknowledgment more than my husband. Without his support and encouragement, this book would have been lost to memory. Thank you, AJ, for your support and your understanding of the time commitment necessary to create this story of our parenting trials and errors. Thank you for holding down the fort at home, with the kids, while I spent hours upon hours writing, editing, re-editing, organizing, and formatting what has become one of my greatest accomplishments, aside from our children. Without you, our family wouldn't exist, and my motivation for writing this book would have waivered and likely disappeared. You are amazing and I love you!

To my children, I love you. Thank you for understanding my reason for spending hours away, and for understanding why I locked myself in the bedroom to write. You all are my inspiration, and motivation to pursue something that at one time seemed bigger than myself. I am so very proud of all of you, and will continue to encourage your growth and guide you toward becoming positive, motivated people and amazing and loving human beings.

Last, I thank my mother. She is the most amazing mother! Her depth of knowledge and experience in raising her six children, and her good sense to share it, prepared me for many experiences as a new mom. She has passed down her wisdom to me, and in writing this book, with her guidance and advice, I am now able to pass on my own wisdom and experiences to my children. Thank you mom...you are priceless!

Blindsided:

To be attacked when vulnerable.

This definition may seem harsh considering that we are talking about, motherhood. However, it is not the child itself that attacks us, but rather the fear, uncertainty, love and new life that leaves us defenseless.

This symbol represents *motherhood*, *family*, and *life*.

It's about learning, adjusting, and enjoying moments. The uphill battle will teach us, the peaks will humble us, the descent will bring joy and peace, and will prepare us for yet another struggle.

Together and individually we will rise, and rise higher. Together and individually we will fall, and fall harder. Together *and* individually we will get back up and keep going.

Introduction

This is good. You've made it this far. You may, however, be thinking that this is just *another* book on parenting. I don't blame you for being skeptical. What do *I* know? What can I say about parenting that the other books haven't already said? I can't give you a simple answer, but I can tell you that this book is genuinely authentic, and straight from delivery!

When I started writing this book I was twenty-eight, and after five years of marriage my husband and I had three children, our youngest being four months old. I was five years into this mother thing but still surprised by each child and wishing that someone had warned me about the information NOT in most parenting books. The nitty and often gritty details and suggestions were very hard to come by, and to my knowledge, didn't even exist in written form.

I didn't realize how valuable this information could be for a mother, especially a brand-new mother, until I experienced "a moment." Jack was four months old, and hungry and ready to eat! I was trying to breastfeed Jack who was crying, pausing, latching on and then quickly pulling away—over and over again. Once again, I felt like a brand-new mom, helpless and frustrated! Finally, after walking and bouncing him for several minutes while cursing him sweetly to myself, it happened! It was that inspiring "moment": the outrageous, unbelievable, adult-like belch that inspired me to write this book! In that moment, I felt an overwhelming responsibility to share with mothers everywhere, all of the information and suggestions

△ *With three children, our youngest being four months old, I had been a mother for five years and was still consistently surprised by each child and wished that someone would have warned me about the information that isn't in most parenting books.*

that I had not been given. At the very least I was set on providing my own children with this information.

At twenty-eight years old, I was a new high school teacher and a mother of three. My children were all under the age of four. Now I am slightly older, with five kids under thirteen and amazingly, I still find a few minutes for myself. Although I've never enjoyed chaos, a messy house, or children crying together like a strategically rehearsed choir, I loved and still love being a mother and I love my children. I hope when you're finished with this book, you will see that I am very normal; I do get frustrated, and at times I feel like I'm going to lose my mind. But I cherish my children, and my responsibility as a parent is serious. My priority is, and always will be, to love them, care for them, teach them and enjoy them.

The idea to write about my experiences started small, as a way to prepare my own children for first-time parenting. I use the word "prepare" very loosely. My plan was to include EVERYTHING, large or small, that I went through as a parent. Beginning with early motherhood, which I think is one of the scariest stages of parenting, to their first day of kindergarten and beyond. The very simple questions become serious issues for the first-time mom.

New grandmas, other moms, and nurses, can give great advice when it comes to the basics. Unless the mother or nurse is a new or recent mom, the information remains only surface level, and may not include the day-to-day of taking care of babies. This is true for most advice: Unless the experience is fresh, it is often diluted or vague.

Setting the Stage

I am the second of six children. We grew up in Northern California, playing sports and staying active. We spent Sundays at church and at home with family. We didn't have a lot, but we had what we needed, including love, family and relationships. Both of my parents come from large families, and all of their siblings have lots of children. This provided us with lots of "friends." A game of wiffle ball fielded completely by cousins under the age of ten was a common activity at our family gatherings. We never moved from our home in rural northern California, and most of us remain in the area.

My husband and I met in high school. We dated through high school and college, and managed to go the distance between California Polytechnic, San Luis Obispo and Santa Clara University for five years. I did most of the travelling, as he was playing college baseball every weekend. We dated over long distances for six years until we were able to get married. The first two years of our marriage, he pursued baseball and sold cars in the off-season, and I finished my teaching credential. We had our two little girls, Ryanne and Reese. Our crazy working family life had begun.

When I had Ryanne, I was very lucky to stay home with her. When Reese came along I was a full-time student. A few years later, I started teaching full-time as an intern, while finishing up my credential classes. After a few years of teaching we had Jack, and I got laid off from my teaching position—in the same month! However, I got a better teaching job at a high school out of town. To say we were busy is an understatement! People, even strangers, would often comment on our children, saying, "Your kids are beautiful," and "boy, you've got your hands full." It's almost as if they could read our minds because they also felt it necessary to remind us to enjoy every stage. This was difficult to do, but we are realizing all too quickly that they don't stay babies forever.

Our family began in 2004 with Ryanne. Now she is thirteen years old, and wise beyond her years, while still acting like a teenager. She is smart, athletic, helpful, responsible, and generous to a fault. She will clean anyone's room if they will let her, just because she wants to. And she'll give her money away faster than she can earn it. She is dramatic and worries more than any young teenager should, as she has been given the genetic gift of anxiety. For now, we keep her busy and emphasize positive thinking, good choices, and yoga!

Reese joined our family in 2005 and is the complete opposite of Ryanne. Although she, too, is smart, athletic and responsible, she's not quite as helpful. It could be the age, as she is eleven. To be fair, she is very helpful when she controls the how and when. Reese wears her heart on her sleeve, but

△ *I do not assume any responsibility for any unsuccessful attempts at "training" your child to sleep, eat, or poop any better than what can be reasonably expected.*

physically she's tough. She loves puppies, and *really* wants one of her own, and she has an inexplicable connection to her baby brothers, although I often see small glimpses of annoyance. And her brother Jack, as far as she's concerned, is the "worst brother ever," and she tells him so. She loves her brother, but we are beginning to feel as if she experiences life differently than the average eleven-year-old girl, and it comes out in frustration and irritation, beyond what is expected. We are now walking the parental discovery road, hoping to uncover a secret that will help us support her.

Jack is our middle child. He is eight and has started third grade. He is one of a kind! His smile—and lisp—will steal your heart. Jack is very caring and full of compliments. He wants to make people smile and feel good. Yes, there's a temper. We've decided not to intervene when sibling disputes get physical, because sometimes he needs to get put in his place. I'm pretty sure most of the time he deserves it!

Jesse is our special angel. He is seven and he is a bundle of joy. Jesse has had lots of physical issues and developmental delays, most of them neurological. To someone on the outside he may look and act like a three-year-old, but to our family he is our special Jesse. His personality is endearing, and he strives to be a part of everything. This amazing little boy can make anyone smile. He's always happy, full of energy, and a reminder of what's important in life. Our family is truly blessed by his existence.

Then there is Joe. Joe completed our family in 2011. He is five and he has a big personality. His sideways glance is hilarious. As Joe grows into his personality, we are reminded of how hard it can be to punish an adorable, silly child without laughing. He's been practicing his lefty golf swing since he was three years old, and is a natural, but at five, Joe is becoming a little too big for his britches. Big brother Jack makes sure to keep him in line. Ah, brotherly love.

Our family is amazing. Our children are awesome—most of the time. Life can get difficult often, but we always try to remember our blessings. Our family does not practice a particular religion, but we do live our life on certain principles. We love our neighbors, so to speak. We cherish our family.

We give service to others, and give back, and we enjoy most things in moderation.

It has been more than ten years since I started writing this book, and we now have five amazing children. Every age brings a new stage of parenting, and parenting will never be mastered—but with the right resources to guide you through them, it can be a much more enjoyable experience. I hope you enjoy this information as much as I have enjoyed sharing it.

Please remember that none of the information you find in this book is scientific. It is not based on any research that I have done, and should not be used for making diagnostic determinations for your children. This book serves mostly as an informative, fun and interesting story of my life as a new mom, that may or may not fill the void of useful motherhood and parenting tips. Enjoy!

△ Notes

One

Preparing For Motherhood

As the seasons change with our children, our responsibilities as parents become more complex. I have five
children between thirteen and five, and every stage with every
one has brought a new surprise. The strategies for teaching
them to live with their habits and their decisions change with
each child at every age. The trickiest stages inevitably involve
a shift in power and independence, which is present at every
age but changes in scope.

For example, kids learn to dress themselves pretty easily,
yet sometimes teaching this skill can be frustrating. Just like
most tasks that involve a surrender of power, this skill can
be considered a healthy habit of independence and not one
of survival. Teaching survival habits is a much tougher feat
in today's world. These habits create life lessons that shape
our children into healthy, responsible and successful adults.
The serious part is that the habits become more influential in
the child's future as he grows. Thankfully, we get to influence
healthy habits and decisions early, taking baby steps to help
prepare us for the more important situations.

When Ryanne was little, we were determined to dress her in
the cutest outfits with matching everything. When she finally
started dressing herself we protested. After all, *what would
other people think if we let her leave the house in that outfit*?
Plaid, stripes and flowers in every color of the rainbow didn't

△ *When Ryanne finally
started dressing herself, we
protested. After all, 'What
would other people think if we
let her leave the house in that
outfit?'*

work for me. It took me much longer than my husband to comfortably allow her to choose her own style. When Reese hit this stage, and was so much more stubborn and specific with her clothing choices, we were so thankful we learned to pick our battles with Ryanne. Ryanne's style was no match for Reese's crazy, eclectic non-matching outfits, and we were no match in fighting with her.

Raising kids is a life of stages and phases. Some are fun and some make you want to lock yourself in your bathroom—forever! It's not always easy or, more accurately, it's rarely easy to be a parent. The moment you figure out her next move is the moment she changes. As our kids grow our parenting responsibilities change and become easier, then more difficult, and then easy again, and so on. Each stage is a new challenge, and most moms will agree with me when I say that there is more to worry about than the terrible twos. I hate to be the bearer of bad news, but parents: Be prepared for "*the terribles*" until your kids graduate from high school. I've only experienced the terrible-twos through thirteen, but most parents of older kids claim that teenagers can be near impossible. Clearly raising kids is never easy. You can't prevent the terribles from happening, or keep your babies from growing into toddlers, teenagers, and adults. However, the more information and even creative ideas you have to work with, the better chance you will have at finding something that works for you and them.

> "Other books had a lot of really good technical information, but I never really wanted to read them. It just seemed too overwhelming. I was looking for real, personal stories, and some guidance on what to do."
>
> — Codi, new mother of 1

So how do you prepare to be a parent? More importantly how can you educate yourself to be a mom? It's tough! I was the first of my friends and siblings to have kids, so to prepare myself I did what most do: I read books. The books I read were mostly helpful as far as what to expect during pregnancy, such as, what happens to your body in month six, or when to call the doctor if you think you're in labor. But they were also a lot like encyclopedias that were sometimes boring and long. I didn't find a lot of the "what to expect from your child as a newborn or toddler," or that I should expect to be sore for two to three weeks after giving birth. No one told me I would be bleeding for six weeks after delivery—although this should have been an obvious side effect. There are a few books in the What to Expect series that address topics specific for the first year, toddlers, and so on. I remember seeing these on the shelves a few years after having Ryanne. These seemed quite long and more technical than what I wanted. My best friend suggested I read *The Girlfriend's Guide to Motherhood*, which she gave me five years too late. I skimmed through this book, only to compare it to mine of course, but never took the time to read it all the way through.

My mom was my book! *But* she forgot to tell me that after giving birth I would be too sore to sit for several weeks—though she did warn me that I wouldn't have milk to feed my baby for the first three to five days. I thought this information quite useful, as did my friends when I shared my experience with them. The most useful advice I got was real information from my mom, and not so much the information I found in the clinical and slightly more scientific, classic motherhood books. I really wasn't excited about reading information from doctors and psychologists, not that these aren't helpful. I was looking for experiences from real moms I could relate to.

> **"I just feel like there is nothing for the first four weeks at all, and all that scientific stuff shouldn't be applied during that time either."**
>
> **— Tawni, new mother of 1**

I relied a lot on my mother's advice, but her memory failed her in the details. I didn't know any better, so when the time came, I thought I was prepared. I expected I would be a natural. I knew how to change a diaper. I'd figure out how to feed her. What else was there? I realized quickly that there is more to motherhood than changing diapers and feeding. What I thought I knew about motherhood hovered around the beautiful, sweet miracle that was my baby. It did not include the blood, stitches, colic, depression, or any of the mess that moms experience. I now realize that being *prepared* for motherhood is a pipe dream. You can try to be ready, and this will help a little, but after five babies of my own, I now know that *prepared* and *motherhood* DO NOT belong together.

> "If I could do it over again, I would pick a class that also included newborn care and 'how to survive on very little sleep.'"
>
> — Theresa, mother of 2

As I explain in the following chapters, the feelings that come with becoming a mother are overwhelming. This is both a wonderful and scary situation. It is such an unexplainable high to bring another human being into the world, and to have the privilege to guide him to adulthood. But feelings of anger, frustration, sadness, and fear can sneak up and create a wave of emotional uncertainty. Understanding this can lower the anxiety just enough to clear your brain for thought, which will be important.

> "I was the first of my friends and family to have a baby, and I had gotten advice for what to expect as far as recovery and new baby stuff, but really had no idea what I was in for!"
>
> — Mama C, new mom

Congratulations on your new baby! Blessings that everything goes as *unexpected* as normal, and that your baby grows up happy and healthy!

△ Notes

Two

Birth and the First Months After

The moment you become a mother is an experience unlike any other. You are blinded by disbelief that you had
anything to do with the creation of another human being and
foggy from the rush of delivery and the mental exhaustion
you feel as you realize she's finally here! Everything that leads
up to those first moments as a mom, from the first sonogram
to finally, her face, has blinded you from the real fact that it's
going to be tough. No matter how prepared you feel you are,
you are in for a ride!

She's here! She's out, and she's all wet! And I'm thinking, *What
is all that icky sticky white stuff?* The doctor laid her on my
tummy, and I stared. I just stared at her, drunk from adrenaline and exhausted from the three-hour pushing marathon
I had just endured. After some time someone, but NOT my
husband, cut the umbilical cord.

This is a vivid memory for me. My husband was not prepared
for the birth and he had to take a few minutes to unwind and
realize that we were ok. Of course he was excited, but he had
been worried about the baby and me. He had stressed himself out and was mentally drained. It's not easy for the dad to
watch his wife or the mother of his child in labor, knowing that
it is still a risk, and still dangerous. He didn't have the strength
to cut the cord, so he let the doctor do it. He did cut one of
our kids' cords, I'm just not sure whose.

△ *If Daddy seems less than
thrilled after delivery, allow
him some time to adjust. He
too has had a life-changing
experience. Reassure him and
ask him how he's doing.*

I've delivered five babies, and all of my deliveries were different. Each one was difficult for my husband to watch. Pain management, in any form, can be helpful for everyone involved, and it was reassuring for my husband because it did help me a little. I had two functional epidurals, a lopsided epidural that numbed my left side but not my right, and an epidural that numbed my face and not my *#@. This was with my first baby, which gave me a very different but realistic experience and expectation of labor and delivery. I was epidural free with Jesse because my labor was only forty-five minutes long, and I was dilated to six before I started. I am not like most women, but fortunately for me I was halfway through dilation before I ever went into labor. Not having an epidural because I didn't have time was horrible! It was awful, painful, unimaginable, BUT, I was quite happy an hour after birth when both my legs worked and I could walk to the bathroom.

My First Delivery

During my first labor, when the epidural numbed the wrong area, I remember thinking *Thank you Lord for ending that misery*! Maybe your delivery will have you singing a different tune like, *that was the most wonderful and harmonious experience I've ever been through*. Whatever the feeling, everything will change with the arrival of your baby. Now you have a brand new baby, *your* baby, on your tummy. You might be wondering, *what do I do now*? Or maybe you're not thinking but completely fixated on every little part of the new little person you've created. From her nose to her toes, she's beautiful and nothing like you could have ever imagined. You no doubt will find yourself staring at every amazing detail of her tiny miraculous little body. You will call her by her name, which will sound very odd at first, but after a week or two, she will start to grow into it. When we called Ryanne by her name when she was just seconds old, we were tempted to change it. It just didn't sound right giving a baby such a grown-up name. We love the name, however, so we allowed ourselves to wonder a little, and kept calling her Ryanne. After a week or two, she really started to become a Ryanne, and it fit her.

After Ryanne was born it took several hours to come down from the high of giving birth. The joy, disbelief, adrenaline, visitors, and everything else that happened within those first few minutes and hours was amazing, but I was exhausted! After the excitement, exhaustion, and/or anesthesia (if you had a C-section), and relief that Ryanne was ok, reality started to set in.

Within the first several minutes after giving birth, my mind was a fuzzy mess of joy and disbelief. I couldn't believe that she was mine. I was a mom! Now what? It was all so surreal, and for a short time, I felt slightly uncomfortable and disconnected from her. Finally, I just relaxed and enjoyed the moment because it's an experience that really can't be described or reproduced. When you give birth to subsequent children, although completely wonderful and equally exciting, the first child is just a different experience because you're a mom for the first time, which is something pretty special.

Some moms don't immediately bond with their babies. It took me a few hours to awake from the dream. If the instant bond isn't there for you, it's ok. Many mothers need some time to adjust. If it takes you more than an instant, a few hours, or even a few days to connect, try not to feel guilty. Some of you may experience a bit of panic over the responsibility of having a baby. It is a huge responsibility to hold a life in your hands. This panic can sometimes distract you from what you are truly feeling, but it's only temporary. How and when you connect with your baby may happen differently than it did for those you know or read about, but it will happen. And the bond will be yours. The chaos of giving birth and anxiety afterward can make it difficult to feel close to your baby, or difficult to feel anything at all, especially from the waist down. But like the epidural, the numbness will subside and you will have a bond with your baby that no one else can share. Be prepared for reality, because it will come soon enough!

△ **TIP:** *Watch the nurses in the hospital. Pay attention to how they handle your newborn. You will learn how tough babies are. This is particularly important for the dads.*

For many new parents, the idea of handling a very small, freshly delivered baby makes them nervous. All they can think of is: "I don't want to hurt her or drop her." This anxiety is normal, but caring for a newborn really isn't as scary as it seems. Paying close attention to the nurses and how they take care of your newborn can ease some anxiety or fear. It will help you understand that babies, although breakable, are really quite tough and resilient. I was given this advice with our second child, and while I didn't fear her size, I needed to remind Daddy of this very true and very helpful consideration. The nurses take care of tiny newborns day in and day out. They're professionals and they're knowledgeable and great at what they do. To a parent with very little or no experience with small babies, nurses may seem rough and careless as they hold, move, reposition, or transition your baby. Take note of this, and you and Daddy will feel more confident when it's your turn. Just remember to carefully support the head and neck, and everything else will likely remain intact. Also know that if you aren't comfortable with baby, he won't be comfortable with you. So cuddle!

With each of our new babies, my husband felt a little uncomfortable. It seemed to take about two weeks for him to loosen up and put his veteran dad hat on. It's easy to forget how resilient babies are because they seem so small and fragile.

Baby's First Night

Expect crying, sleeping, and lots of funny noises. Yes, newborns sound a lot like squeaking animals of all sorts, and it can be troubling, not to mention make it very difficult to sleep. I didn't sleep much my first night as a mom. Every little squeak or whimper prompted me to sit up or roll over to make sure she was okay. After Jack, I was asking the nurses to take him out so I could sleep. Although the noises no longer worried me, they made sleeping impossible. He was so noisy! I also knew what to expect and that sleep would not happen if he stayed. Once we left the hospital, we were on our own. Some might disagree with my decision to remove the noisy little guy. How could I let them take the baby away!? Well, after five kids I realize more than ever that sleep is essential for caring for a newborn, and a family. You have to take care of *you* first, and sleep should be a top priority. I felt confident my baby would be fine without me for an hour or two, especially in the hands of skilled and experienced nurses. Removing my new one from my room was difficult to do but as you will soon realize,

△ **FYI:** *Newborns sound a lot like squeaking animals of all sorts, and it can be troubling, not to mention make it very difficult to sleep.*

in parenting, difficult decisions are around every corner! From day one, life with kids is never easy.

Don't feel bad if you want a little rest without your baby. You're not a bad mom, or dad, if you have the nurses take him for a few hours at a time. They will bring him in so you can breastfeed. Sometimes it's easier for you if the nurses keep the baby. They come in so often that first night to retrieve the baby for tests that it's not a bad idea to try to sleep for a few hours at a time. When it's your first child, of course, you'll probably be content taking turns holding and staring at your new one all night long.

Our first night in the hospital was a bit overwhelming. We wanted to hold her and just stare at her for hours. We didn't want to miss anything! We were all over every whimper and every diaper change. None of our babies cried a lot the first night in the hospital, which helped a little. Instead, what I remember most about them all, and what kept me awake more than anything, was the spitting up and the sound of choking soon after. Typically, brand new infants don't spit up a lot, but they do have phlegm and amniotic fluid, and it starts to make its way out soon after birth. It's very scary to hear your baby choking, but it's no emergency. After I realized this was normal, and knew how to handle it, I simple turned Baby over onto her side and patted her back until she seemed better. You can imagine how much sleep you might get if your baby "chokes" every thirty minutes, and you're worried about her doing it again all the minutes in between. It was pretty exhausting for both of us the first night and days after birth. Mom, you'll be up every few hours, and you will be exhausted, emotional, unsure, and uncomfortable. But Dad will be tired, too. He might also feel a little grumpy and left out. Remember to help each other through the first few weeks, because you both will be very emotional, and arguments will likely ensue.

In the weeks leading up to the birth, your bulging, swollen and hormonal body has allowed you to adjust to a lack of sleep. You are used to getting by with little sleep, so the transition from being pregnant to new mom is much easier for you. The transition for dads isn't as easy. Many will break emotionally from a lack of sleep. It might show up within the first week,

△ *TIP: When you hear what sounds like choking from your infant, simply turn Baby over onto her side and pat her back until she seems better.*

and it might be in the form of irritability, crying, a lack of involvement, or in many other forms. But it's important for them that we notice.

Recovery After Baby Number One

With baby number one I was extremely sore "down there" for two weeks. I couldn't sit on a soft couch without cringing for a good five days. My leg muscles were sore from all the slow up-and-down squatting I did to get on and off the couch. I had a normal delivery with no complications, but I did push for almost three hours. Apparently, I had really strong muscles that didn't want to stretch.

△ **FYI:** *With subsequent deliveries, the pain lessons dramatically, and recovery time is much quicker.*

Have you ever heard the theory that being in shape makes labor easier? Well, this is true in the sense that you have more energy to easily endure a long, hard labor. When it comes time to push, the in-shape moms are ready and willing with energy to spare, while those that are not as active often let exhaustion get the best of them. Unfortunately, being in good shape also means your muscles don't have the give to allow your baby an easy exit. Although strong muscles get you through labor and make it easier to push the baby out, your muscles don't stretch. If the pushing stage of labor takes awhile, make sure you assume it's because your muscles are in great shape!

As I was saying, I had some pretty decent tears in my muscles, which is normal, and something to expect. Don't be surprised if you can't sit down for a week. Be patient because it will get better and easier. It took about two weeks before I felt comfortable sitting. When I was in the hospital, the nurses gave me ice packs for my soreness, and I'm sure this is a common practice. These homemade ice packs were diapers that had been cut down the center and filled with crushed ice. They were soft, cold, and absorbent, and it really helped with the soreness. My advice is to ask for these for as long as you are in the hospital. The nurses may tell you that the ice packs work for only the first few hours, but whether they work for swelling, or just feel good, it doesn't matter. Ask for them! And don't be afraid to ask for anything else you might need.

Hemorrhoid creams or pads were also good at relieving some of the burning.

> **"In the first few weeks, I was afraid to pee in public without my squirt bottle."**
> — Codi, new mother of 1

Some good news to report is that with subsequent deliveries, the pain lessons dramatically, and recovery time is much quicker. So, if you're planning on having more than one, know that your "area" will feel much better the second time around.

The nurses will most likely warn you about blood clots. If they don't, however, expect that you will have blood clots! You will pass them for several days after delivery. They are gross in every way possible. They are big, even golf ball-sized, but they get smaller and smaller as each day passes. If they are larger than a golf ball, you need to let someone know. I was so grossed out after a few of these it was hard to look. The nurses warned me, but I was not prepared! So, expect them. I would recommend wearing Spandex shorts, or firm-fitting underwear for the first week, if you can handle it. If you can imagine having a really heavy period, and only using pads, each time you stand up you feel it, and you end up grabbing your crotch as you're standing up and walking to and from the bathroom. The crotch grabbing, in case you were wondering, is an attempt to lesson the gush of blood. Snug-fitting Spandex will simulate the crotch grabbing by pushing the pad against you so the feeling isn't as strong. Sadly, nothing will eliminate the gush completely. I wore comfortable, yet firm-fitting Spandex with my last two, and it helped tremendously.

Something else to look forward to is constipation. For the first few days to a week, it is very likely you will need stool softeners. Do not leave the hospital without them! These are absolutely necessary and you will be miserable if you leave empty handed. If you don't use them, fine, but if you don't have them, you'll have to wait for them, and it won't be pretty, or fun. With my second child, Reese, I was not given a

△ **TIP:** *Spandex shorts or firm-fitting underwear for the first week or two can really help with the uncomfortable gushing.*

△ *With my second child, Reese, I was not given a prescription for stool softeners and I forgot, or maybe I was too embarrassed to ask for them. Four days later, I was so miserable and uncomfortable that I spent hours in the bathroom only to produce a few tears and a very sore rear end.*

prescription for stool softeners and I forgot, or maybe I was too embarrassed to ask for them. Four days later, I was so miserable and uncomfortable that I spent hours in the bathroom only to produce a few tears and a very sore rear end.

> "This is something I have never experienced until I had my first child, and let me tell you it felt like I was pushing out another baby! I had to figure out the hard way that stool softeners will become your best friend. With baby number two, I did not leave without them!"
>
> — Jessica, mother of 2

The first few weeks after delivery will be pretty miserable. You'll be exhausted and very sore, breastfeeding or not, your breasts will be engorged like balloons inflated to their limits. Oh, and don't forget the new life for which you are now responsible—she keeps crying and you don't know how to make her stop. Your husband, or the father, will likely feel left out and a little ignored, and may seem a little distant. His adjustment to the baby will be more difficult than yours, so it's important that you try to involve him as much as possible. Luckily, the excitement of new motherhood and parenthood will make adjusting to all the "discomforts" much easier, and you probably won't notice how beat up you feel.

> "When we got home from the hospital, I was not prepared for the surge of emotions I had. I sat down and sobbed uncontrollably for a while. Everything had changed and it was overwhelming."
>
> — Kara, new mother of 1

Again, be prepared for reality! It sets in as soon as you leave the hospital and are in the car, driving home. You will no doubt be driving ten miles per hour, and yelling at Daddy every time he takes a sharp turn. Once you get home, you may feel a little anxious about being on your own. But again, trust your instincts. The first few to four or five weeks with Baby may follow a pretty predictable schedule: feeding, sleeping (for you and baby), diaper changing, and repeat. Throw in a few crying episodes for you and Baby just to keep it predictable. Then, if she doesn't cry, you have it made! As long as she's fed, changed, and rested, the crying generally doesn't mean anything. So stay calm and just be with her.

It took me about two weeks to start feeling normal, physically, and a little longer to adjust to motherhood. It was about six weeks when I really began to adjust to *all* the new changes. After six weeks, the new baby, my new boobs, and my new life were very normal. The bleeding had stopped completely and it felt as if my life had never been any different. After talking to many new moms, six weeks seems to be the magic number. You will feel pretty tired and awkward, and probably like you will never be normal. By six weeks, you will find a groove, and start to feel comfortable in your new reality.

Cesarean Recovery

Recovery after having a cesarean section is a bit different. I do not have experience with this, but I know a few friends who do, and they shared some of their experiences with me. Here are some of the things you can expect with a cesarean.

There are two different cesarean procedures—emergency and scheduled. In an emergency situation, anesthesia is absolutely necessary. It can affect your whole body, but the numbness affects the lower half of the body for several hours after the procedure. You may be groggy when you come out of it, and it is likely you will need a lot of help within the first twenty-four hours. Your lower half will be numb, requiring a catheter and extra help from the nurses. After twenty-four hours you may be asked to get up and walk, which could be painful in the ab-domen, and also in your neck and shoulders. The anesthetic gas can move into muscle tissue and cause pain, resulting in full body pain and discomfort. Bloating can be severe and long lasting, as a result of the pumping of air into the abdomen to make room for Baby during the procedure. The incision area will also be very sore. Most cesareans require a three day stay in the hospital, but depending on Mom and Baby, it could be longer.

In the emergency scenario, the initial muscle pain from the anesthesia, bloating in the abdomen, and pain from the incision can last for several weeks. What makes all of this worse is that you are now caring for a newborn—waking at night, putting pressure on your incision when breastfeeding, highly hormonal, and experiencing vaginal bleeding. What?! Moms that deliver via c-section still go through the six week vaginal bleeding and recovery?! I was surprised to hear this, although it makes sense—it just doesn't seem fair.

> **"When we got home from the hospital it was a lot harder than I thought it would be. Breastfeeding was difficult, and my hormones were completely in control. It also got really hard on my husband, a week after, because he realized he was getting zero of my attention and that it wasn't just about him anymore. We fought, and that was hard."**
>
> — Mama C, new mom

A scheduled cesarean typically happens on subsequent deliveries, after having had a cesarean with the first delivery. Although I have heard that moms are asking for a cesarean so they can avoid the vaginal delivery. Again I say, *"What?! Why would anyone want to have someone cut open their stomach if it wasn't absolutely necessary?"* Similar to delivery and recovering from a second baby, the recovery from a planned cesarean is much shorter and easier. The hospital stay is shorter, the bloating is much less, there is very little if any muscle pain, and the incision is less sensitive and painful. However, the vaginal bleeding still happens, unfortunately.

In addition to a longer and more intense recovery after having a cesarean, you may also be given certain restrictions on activity, lifting (not on weight lifting, hehe, but no weight lifting either), and an extended period of waiting before exercising.

Instead of six weeks post baby, it could be eight weeks or longer. Recovery may seem years away but like most things, you will get there. Try to ask for the help you need, learn to listen to your body, and give yourself the extra attention you need and deserve.

Don't Forget Daddy

In the first few days, weeks, and even months of our babies' lives my husband had a difficult time connecting. He would say, "He's so tiny, I don't want to hurt him." It was even harder for him to bond since he wasn't the one who delivered the baby! He wasn't the one nursing every two or three hours. But he wanted to be very involved and he did whatever he could to connect with them early on.

When Ryanne was first born, my husband struggled to connect with her, and it was difficult for him to adjust to our new life as parents. The first week was very rough. Neither of us got much sleep, if any, the first few nights, and severe exhaustion really got to him. He was grumpy and distant, and seemed like he felt a little left out. After talking with several moms with similar experiences, it seems common for the dads to feel slightly abandoned and alone.

△ *The transition period for dads is much shorter. It starts with the first contraction and it ends with the last push. They go from husband to dad in a matter of hours.*

"My husband said he did not realize how much harder having a baby would be on our relationship."

— Mama K, new mom

If you think about it, new mothers are exhausted and sore from labor. We are learning to breastfeed, we're tired from a lack of sleep, and we're emotionally drained. All our attention and energy is going toward taking care of the baby. We are distant, and have been since month seven of our pregnancy when we began to get uncomfortable. We've been adjusting to motherhood since early pregnancy, and are much more prepared mentally for the new arrival. The transition period for dads is much shorter. It starts with the first contraction and it ends with the last push. They go from husband to dad in a matter of hours and this can be emotionally overwhelming and extremely scary. Combine this with a severe lack of sleep and what you get is a cranky, moody, distant husband or partner who isn't sure how to deal with it all.

As tough as it might be, it's really important to support your partner and encourage his involvement. Try to make him feel important to you and your new family, and be sensitive to his needs. Some needs will seem unimaginable, as I'm sure you can guess what "needs" I'm referring to. These are completely out of the question for the first six weeks. Ouch! It may be much longer for some. Be sensitive to the things you can give him and try to understand how he feels. After a few weeks, you both will be much more comfortable and prepared, and he will slowly start to involve himself in the everyday activities.

> **"My husband told me one day that having a baby was easier than he thought it would be. I couldn't decide if I wanted to punch him or cry."**
>
> **— Codi, new mother of 1**

In the process of going from one kid to five, my husband has involved himself in as many activities as possible. Early on, his job was bottle-feeding. Then he called dibs on changing diapers. He got pretty good at it and I think he just liked to brag: "Wow, that was a five wiper, but I got it in two!" After five, he became a pro changer. Just ask him! Moms, do not let Dad get out of this part! It's his baby too, and changing diapers is a huge part of parenting and raising a child! If he can handle poop, he really should take on diaper changing. All dads need ways to feel close to their new babies, so changing diapers is perfect! (Wink, wink) They can also do some bottle-feeding, baths, and a multitude of other things. In my opinion, they should step up in all things!

Together, we came up with ways for my husband to be involved with all our babies. It was tough when they were all just weeks old, because they were so small and seemed so fragile. To be honest, he didn't feel comfortable and connected with any of them until they were about three months old.

Developing daily routines or rituals can really help to connect them. My husband's favorite thing to do with our babies was always sleeping with them on our couch or recliner. They loved it, too, because they would sleep for hours on his chest. This is how he bonded with each of them, and it became a routine that brought him very close with our kids.

> "It's easy to let the relationship fall a bit, with both parents sleep deprived, stressed, and uncertain. A friend told us to be kind to each other, and surrender to the process. This was great advice."
>
> — Kara, new mother of 1

Nighttime Feedings

Ideally, you will be waking at night to feed your baby for only the first three or four months. It might be every two hours, or it might be slightly longer, if you're lucky. I say *ideally* because many babies continue waking at night, long after they reach three or four months, but this is the time when they start to sleep longer and are more able to sleep all night. This is when I stopped feeding all my babies, except for little Jess man. He was different.

How early you eliminate the nighttime feedings depends on a lot of things. Only you and your baby can determine when it's time. But when you are approaching this milestone, remember this one little question: *When will I need a full night's sleep and when does my baby need it?*

From day one you will be waking to feed your baby. There are a lot of routines that can help you get through each nighttime feeding. Many choose to bring Baby into bed and "sleep-feed." If you're not familiar with "sleep-feeding," it's very similar to

△ **FYI:** *Eliminating a nighttime feeding involves this important question: When will I need a full night's sleep and when does my baby need it?*

sleep walking, except that you are laying down and sleeping (not actually sleeping), and breastfeeding without knowing it. Okay, so this is a joke. I think a better term would be passive feeding, because it's happening, but you are not actively engaged. But seriously, the baby gets good at latching on in the horizontal position, and you get very good at nursing without hands, and without conscience, really. Baby gets fed, and you get sleep. Sounds great! It isn't, and it will create a very difficult habit to break. I was never very good at passive feeding, although I tried and tried, but after a few kids, I was thankful for this failure.

For every nighttime feeding I got completely out of bed. I sat in a chair right next to my bed, and I made it very accommodating for breastfeeding. It was my area, my zone, and it was handy and mostly comfortable. I never used a nursing stool, but if you breastfeed in a chair or on a couch, I would suggest getting one. I was constantly moving pillows, laundry baskets, or stuffed animals to prop my feet and knees up, and give me more support during breastfeeding. Without it I often felt uncomfortable.

> "Nighttime feedings were so hard. I found that I got way over tired after just a couple of nights of feeding. I ended up co-sleeping a lot in the beginning, without a shirt on — just because I needed sleep so much!"
>
> — Chrystina, mother of 3

Every night for the first three months I sat in a chair fully awake, and breastfed every three to four hours. I felt I needed to be awake as much as Baby. I started on one breast and nursed as long as Baby needed. I often undressed my babies down to their diaper to wake them or keep them awake during feeding. I realized early that if they fell asleep too soon, they wouldn't get satisfied and then would wake up sooner to eat more. This seems to happen to a lot of moms that feed passively. My friends used to talk often about their passive feeding habits and being awake all night because their babies were always hungry. Their babies would nurse themselves just enough until they fell back to sleep, and continued this cycle every hour. It's kind of like sucking on a binkie. It doesn't fill the tummy, but soothes the soul. Can you see why I wasn't disappointed when I did not master the art of sleep feeding? I didn't seem to have trouble with my babies waking every one to two hours at night. Generally, they woke up every three hours like clockwork, but I tried to hold them off to every four hours.

After feeding on the first side I burped them for at least five minutes. If I didn't, they would usually spit up and almost always all over themselves or their bed. Sometimes I laid them down on a blanket on the bed (my changing table), and then picked them up again. For some reason, this up down movement seemed to move the air and milk, and helped them burp and spit up. And because I expected it, I was able to guide the spit up to my shoulder instead of all over them. The last thing you want to do is change an entire outfit in the middle of the night because they are soaked from spit up.

I almost always changed the diaper in between the right and left breasts. To be clear, after breast-feeding on the right breast, I burped, changed the diaper, swaddled tightly, and then breast-fed on the left side. All this usually kept awake, or woke up, Baby to nurse more on the second side. After the second side or when my baby fell asleep, I would do a gentle burping and put him in his bassinet with a binkie close by. I always kept a burp rag underneath the baby's head to avoid any spit up from soaking into his hair. This is safe to do when your little guy or gal doesn't move a lot.

So what do you do if you get Baby fed, changed, and swaddled, and he decides to blow it out his shorts as soon as you put him in his bed, or right after you swaddle him? I remember this happening three out of four nights with all of my babies. With my first child, I unwrapped and woke her, opened the diaper, and found...almost nothing in there. What sounded like fireworks was usually nothing. My point: As long as the black poop is out, there is no need to wake your baby to change her diaper when she poops—you'll risk waking her or wasting a diaper. New babies don't poop a lot at a time, so let her

△ *What do you do if you get Baby fed, changed, and swaddled, and he decides to blow it out his shorts as soon as you put him in his bed, or right after you swaddle him? Do you change him?*

sleep and rest assured that she will be just fine with poop in her diaper. In the first few months it's the soggy diapers you need to worry about and not so much the poopy ones. Pee-soaked diapers cause leakage on Baby's clothes, your clothes, and bedding, creating more changing and laundry for you. It also encourages a moist environment, which isn't always comfortable. So change a soggy diaper and let the poopy ones be, at least at night when they're sleeping.

Within the first few days of birth, check the diaper often, morning, noon, and night, until all of the icky black poop called meconium, has been eliminated. When it comes out, it often has no sound nor odor so it can catch you by surprise. But don't let it! There is nothing worse than finding sticky, black poop attached to both the diaper and the delicate skin of your baby. You don't want to have to "unstick" your baby's ball sack from a diaper or his own leg. This happened to me, and I was horrified! And it happened with Joe, the *baby* baby! You'd think I would have been prepared for this but it hadn't happened before, that I could recall, so why would I have thought of it. Plus, being a veteran mom I sometimes paid less attention to the details of caring for a newborn. It backfired, and I was caught off guard! So, another important reason for this book is to warn you about ball sacks and sticky poop! They don't mix! And to remind you to check and change baby diapers often within the first days of birth.

Care of the Umbilical Cord

The doctors and nurses don't always tell you how to take care of the umbilical cord before you go home. I did different things with each of my kids. Actually, what I should say is that I got less and less concerned about taking care of it at all. With Ryanne, the doctors told me to clean the area with alcohol at every diaper change. So, I did. Then with Reese they didn't really tell me anything, so I cleaned the area with alcohol a few times a day. And, of course, with Joe, the neglected child, I cleaned the area with water once or twice a day. All three "methods" produced the same result—a clean, dry scab that fell off after about two weeks. I can say that it took longer for Jesse's umbilical cord to fall off than the others, but this was a

△ *There is nothing worse than finding sticky, black poop attached to both the diaper and the delicate skin of your baby. You don't want to have to "unstick" your baby's ball sack from a diaper or his own leg. This happened to me, and I was horrified!*

muscle development and delay issue, and some kids just take longer to do things! Whatever the case, keeping it clean and allowing it to stay dry and friction free (keeping the diaper folded and below the area) is the best way to take care of it, so don't stress too much about it.

Circumcision

If you have a boy and decide to get him circumcised, don't watch. Although a very interesting procedure, it can be somewhat traumatizing because it looks much worse than it really is. The baby is screaming (more from having his legs strapped down than from pain), and it's difficult to watch. It is a quick procedure and your son will recover emotionally, pretty quickly. The physical recovery is much more difficult, but again, more for you than the baby.

You will be changing diapers four to six times a day, at least, and each time you change him you also will be caring for the circumcised area. It looks disgusting, and very painful, and slightly gooey. But, it's just one more thing you'll be taking care of in the first few weeks. You will be very glad when the cord has fallen off, and the bandage can come off of the baby's "pee pee" (typically seven to ten days following the procedure).

△ **FYI:** *Beware of getting peed on and baby erections. They do happen.*

> "I was surprised how motherly instincts really do kick in and you know what your child needs. I can't get over how much I love watching his development, and mine."
>
> — Mama K, new mom

There are different types of procedures for circumcision. The wound and healing depends on how it is done. You will likely get a handout from the doctor before you go home. When caring for the area, you may need to put Vaseline on the circumcised area and the diaper to prevent sticking. After seven to ten days, you can remove the bandage. Beware of its appearance. It will still look disgusting and be very sore, but this is normal. It may look a little funny for a while but it will eventually start to look like a real penis.

It is very likely you will come across a baby erection. This is strange no question, and can be a little disturbing at first. It is quite normal and can be very funny. Also, baby boys have a tendency to pee as soon as the diaper comes off. Have a towel handy or something to cover his penis. There are products like the Peepee Teepee, which was created for this reason. It is not all that effective in absorption or prevention, but the idea is quite amusing and it can lighten the moment if and when you are getting peed on. My daughter will agree that having a blocking tool is important.

Early after Joe was born, Ryanne was helping me change his diaper. It was more like smiling and distracting him. I was in the changing position and she was at his head, looking over him making faces. Two seconds after the diaper came off he peed—straight over his head and right at Ryanne's face! I think it even got in her mouth. She was horrified and is likely a little scarred too! Needless to say, she changed her positioning for future diaper changes.

△ *I was in the changing position, and Ryanne was at his head, looking over him, making faces. Two seconds after the diaper came off he peed—straight over his head and right at Ryanne's face! I think it even got in her mouth.*

DIAPERING TIPS

△ Waiting to change a diaper until it is full of pee is ok. Disposable diapers are so absorbent, and they keep moisture off your baby. It's better for the environment (although not as good as cloth, of course) and your wallet. Poop, however, is a different story.

△ Don't be stingy with the diaper rash cream or ointment. A thick layer for a week will clear up the blistering and peeling of a severe rash. It needs to be thick enough to protect against any moisture.

△ Essential oils like lavender can help clear a diaper rash and soothe the burning.

△ Try using a warm rag instead of a wipe if you start to see redness on the rear. Wipes can irritate sensitive baby skin, causing stinging and worsening rash.

△ Diaper bag basics should always include diapers, wipes, rash cream, burp rags, and at least two clean outfits. It's very possible for a baby to wet or ruin two outfits within minutes. You will also want to include an extra shirt for yourself.

After the adjustment period subsides and you've survived all the firsts of early parenting, you begin using your natural parenting skills. After the first six weeks, it becomes very important to start thinking about and implementing routines and schedules. You are feeling more normal, physically, and your mind and body have adjusted to the lack of sleep. It's now

MY CLOTHING ESSENTIALS FOR BABY

Some of the cutest outfits for babies are the most uncomfortable, and they also make it difficult to hold your child. Some of them make changing a diaper a real challenge. Here are my clothing essentials that are comfortable for Baby and you, as well as outfits that I would have avoided, had I known better.

△   Onesies are the best! These were my favorite outfits in the summer, and in winter, they work great under sweatsuits and sleepers, or anything considered winter wear.

△   Sleepers (warm one piece) are great for winter. They are easy to get on/off and are comfortable for wearing and make it easier for holding Baby.

△   One piece outfits, or rompers are wonderful for summer or warmer weather.

△   T-shirts are great when babies are older and sitting up.

△   Choose shoes with soft, flexible soles such as Robeez®. Hard, rubber-soled shoes are expensive, don't stay on, and are uncomfortable. Plus they are worn only a few times, because kids grow extremely fast.

△   Lots and lots of socks. Tight fitting, high crew socks work well. A little stretch in the fabric helps them stay on better than all cotton. I recommend the Hanes® brand or Circo® brands from Target.

△   Avoid dresses and lots of frills for girls (and boys too!). Although adorable and hard to resist, they are not comfortable.

△   Overalls and shirts with collars or zippers are no good. When they are very little, the collar will ride up and they will eat it! The overall straps sometimes poke and rub into baby's neck and mouth. Overalls become more practical (and adorable) when they're walking or even sitting up. This is the same for zip-up sweatshirts.

time to start guiding and encouraging your baby to develop good, healthy habits. And it's time for you to start thinking about an easier life for you, Dad, and Baby. Take note of the previous page for some other things I've learned.

It's amazing how you begin your journey as a mother feeling so many changes all at once. Emotion and physical discomforts can have you believing that you will never be normal. Hang in there! You will soon be parenting subconsciously, and will feel like a pro! Well, you may not feel like a pro, but you won't be as concerned that you are doing it all wrong, or that you are making mistakes that will permanently damage your child.

△ Notes

Three

Postpartum Depression

Early after delivering a baby, and very soon into your new life as a mom, the baby blues will likely visit you. Also called postpartum depression, these experiences can really run you through the ringer. The emotional highs and lows that are typical with new moms never feel like they belong or that they are normal. But they are.

It's different for every mom but a little bit of sadness and some crying can be expected. You may even have moments of anger and frustration, but again, every mom is different, and it is normal.

Common experiences in my early postpartum days involved tears shed for a TV commercial that had nothing to do with anything. Some were outbursts of anger with a little bit of yelling. You may even feel depressed and down. Remember, it is very normal so you shouldn't feel ashamed. Your hormones are so out of control, especially early on, and your body isn't sure how to handle it. Talk with other moms, friends, or family about how you feel. Talk with your husband or partner. You are a wonderful, caring mother who "grew a baby" as my daughter would say, for nine months, and your body is adjusting without it. It's also preparing for your baby's survival by producing milk, which can keep your hormones on edge for as long as you breastfeed. You may feel embarrassed about how you feel. Don't be afraid to talk to someone. It is much

△ *The emotional highs and lows that are typical with new moms never feel like they belong or that they are normal. But they are.*

more common than most people realize, and knowing you're not alone can really ease the worry, embarrassment, and even shame you might be feeling.

Trying to rationalize your feelings might only make you feel worse. I remember heavy periods of sadness that completely overwhelmed my early days as a new mom. I tried to understand why I felt the way I did, and it only made me feel worse. I thought, *I should be feeling happy. Why am I so sad?* And, of course, this made me feel guilty, so I became more depressed and sad, and I was embarrassed to talk about it. So I didn't. After our second baby the sadness came back, along with a little anger and frustration, because now we had a toddler *and* a new baby. I talked with my husband and it helped. He said I should also talk with my mom and friends who would be able to relate and comfort me a little. I did, and the weight of guilt was lightened. The guilt that comes from feeling unhappy about being a mom can push you further into a depression that may not go away. Find an outlet and reach out to it.

"I knew something was off after my second child was born. I knew how I was supposed to be, but having to force myself to be normal was overwhelming. I looked back after my daughter was about one and then realized what had happened. I'm not sure many noticed my signs of postpartum depression, but I dealt with it alone."

— Jennifer, veteran mother of 3

It's possible that your "depression" will last for much longer than a few days. Technically, it is no longer called the baby blues but I'd have to call it the crazy life blues. From my first pregnancy to my last, my emotions were a lot like an upside down roller coaster — fast, slow, and out of control. The pregnancy and post-delivery hormones can last a really long time, and these hormones created a vicious cycle that confused my body and mind. As I kept having babies, my body was continuously adapting to pregnancy and breastfeeding.

As our family grew, life became more complicated and stressful. It took me years to realize that I would be experiencing the emotional ups and downs as long as my body was undergoing its constant fluctuations. This is not scientific information. It is how I felt. I strongly believed it would take some time, years even, for my body and hormones to return to normal once I stopped having babies, and only time would tell me. The baby stage may be ending for me, but as our kids get older, life offers them more opportunities, and with this comes added stress. Taking an antidepressant, although not my first choice, was a good way for me to start my battle with overactive hormones. My first preference is and always will be to work to restore the balance naturally, and to combat a stressful life through other methods such as diet, exercise, relaxation and vitamins. I don't like taking drugs and there are alternatives.

> "We were four months into this parenting thing and it was still tough to surrender to our new life. I had horrible anxiety the first trip we took, and we were just going to my hometown to visit my parents! I was so uncomfortable and worried about the baby the whole time, that I couldn't involve myself in the conversations."
>
> — Mama K.S., new mom

I didn't start taking antidepressants until after Reese, our second, was about six months old. After she was born, I really had a difficult time feeling happy. My moods were very up and down. One day I felt blessed and overjoyed at how lucky I was and the next day I was irritable, moody, and easily frustrated. It was completely unlike me. And with each child and pregnancy it seemed to get worse. Could it be that with each child, life gets faster, busier, and more stressful?

When Jack was a year old I started taking Zoloft regularly. I had become a "loose canon," never knowing when I was going to fire. Frustration came so easily and suddenly, and I could never really pinpoint the cause. I finally realized that it was never really one thing that set me off, but my unpredictable mood, my frame of mind, and my situation. Taking medication, although difficult at first, really helped me feel normal. Alternatives to prescription medication such as yoga, meditation, message therapy, and vitamin and herbal supplements, can also work, and I recommend trying these first. They can be time-consuming and expensive, but they are a healthier and more enjoyable way of coping with post-baby blues, and the stress of everyday life with kids. Getting out around other adults for conversation can also help lift your mood.

Getting Active

When I found out I was pregnant with Joe, I stopped taking an antidepressant. After Joe was born I started it again. Five kids can really drive a parent nuts! I stayed on an antidepressant for a few years after Joe was born, but I made exercise a priority in my weekly routine. I've really noticed the benefits, both physically and emotionally, since getting active again. It is now becoming a hobby I can share with my kids, as they get older. It is possible and much easier to stay home! You don't need a gym. If you get the right workout program at home, it's easy to fit in ten, twenty, or thirty minutes of a workout. It's not only good for you but as your kids get older, they will want to join in. They will learn about good health by example, and will begin to understand how important it is to stay fit and exercise. Kids learn so many things by the example of their parents. This one is so important that it might help balance out the habits you're teaching of which you might not be so proud. Or we can only hope.

△ If an antidepressant is the first step in your plan, it doesn't have to be the last.

Once I decided to get active again, my determination stayed. I even finished my first half marathon, and was able to train and run with my daughter, who also enjoys running and exercise. How I found the time to train and get back in to exercise, I'm not sure. It has a lot to do with my part-time teaching schedule, and a beautiful river trail right next to my school. I also made a decision to do it, which made all the difference in keeping to a regimen and making it happen. Not everybody has the opportunities I did, but it is important to come up with a plan and stick to a routine, if getting active is your goal. If an antidepressant is the first step in your plan, it doesn't have to be the last.

> "I've always struggled with anxiety but did not feel *any* during pregnancy. After my daughter was born, about the time my milk came in, my anxiety came back with a vengeance! I worried something would happen to my daughter, or to me, and that my baby and her dad would have to live without me. I take DHA supplements and these really help with my anxiety. Cardio also helps me tons! Relaxation and yoga is not something that I can do — the harder I work, the better I feel."
>
> — Mama CC, new mom

If you are feeling this way and can identify that the cause is "mood swings" and/or hormones, talk with your husband about it. If he doesn't know where your "rages" and "meltdowns" are coming from, he may think it's him (and maybe it is). He might think you're going crazy! He may also feel it necessary to put up his guard and fight back, making you even more frustrated and upset. Tell him how you're feeling, and explain how "out of control" or sad you feel. He needs to know what's going on so that he can try to understand — and hopefully will not upset you when you are most vulnerable. Good, productive communication with your spouse is extremely important. Talk it out so both of you understand one another.

A Costco Trip Gone Horribly Awry

I remember, specifically, a hormonal episode that happened when Joe was four months old. I can't explain it other than to say it was my monthly Costco trip gone horribly awry. My list was long and my time was limited—not uncommon in my life. It was after work and I had an appointment for Jesse that I couldn't miss. Plus, my boobs were full of milk because I had just cut out a feeding/pumping and my body was still adjusting. I was in a hurry.

I sped through, grabbing things quickly and dodging carts. I checked and rechecked my list of essentials, double checking that I had grabbed the birthday cookies for Ryanne and her class, for the next day. Racing to the register, I gave my card and reusable Costco bags to the clerk. Seconds after scanning my card, I saw that the register said "See Bank." This short but very powerful alert put me into shock, as this had never happened to me. I didn't have checks and without my American Express, I was unable to pay. I stood there for what seemed like ten minutes and then I called my husband. No answer. I called my mother-in-law, the V.P. of my bank. No answer. Tears of shock and embarrassment started to come slowly. Leaving with nothing meant I had just wasted an hour of my life, and this made me cry. I had filled my own bags, so walking out meant leaving without them, and unpacking them would have made a scene. This too, made me cry. I tried calling again, but again no answer. I cried.

An employee finally came over to "rescue me," but she couldn't help because I had lost all ability to rationalize the situation, and anything and everything she tried either failed, or made me more upset. I was now crying my eyes out completely embarrassed, and unable to gain my composure, so I finally decided to leave. I unpacked my bags as quickly as possible, paid for a twenty-four-pack of chocolate chip cookies with the cash I had brought, and left. I cried to the car, and the entire thirty-minute drive home. Thinking back several weeks later I wondered, WHY? What made me so upset at such a silly situation?

Well, initially, every time I relived the situation, it made me sad. Sadness for the hour of lost time, sadness for missing Jesse's appointment, and sadness for getting so sad. Looking back, I realized that my hormones were to blame. Still completely irregular, and with boobs full of milk, my body was an unpredictable mess! The sadness remained still, a week later when I brought my husband a burrito for lunch. I forgot to get salsa and clearly, he was disappointed. I cried! He wasn't mean, or condescending, or very upset at all. But I cried! I remember crying on several occasions for weeks after that Costco trip. But then, it went away, and constant sadness was replaced by only periods of sadness and frustration.

△ *"Still completely irregular and with boobs full of milk, my body was constantly changing and adjusting. These fluctuations brought tears with ANY unexpected dilemma I encountered."*

Another vivid memory involves peeling eggs! Have you ever tried peeling an egg, and ended up taking off half the egg white along with the shell? Well, my eggs, more often than not, are difficult to peel. As I started peeling the first egg, I hoped and prayed that it was going to be easy. My daughter was waiting for an egg sandwich, patiently at first, and then less patient as time passed. The eggs weren't cooperating and I became extremely frustrated at the eggs for not peeling! My husband looked at me like I was crazy, as I was nearly screaming at the darn things. It took all I had to avoid giving my kids a very unnecessary vocabulary lesson on expletives. All I wanted to do was throw the thing across the room, and break it against the wall! What the heck was happening to me!?

Well, of course it had to be hormones. My rationale was always hormones. Hormones can do incredible things to otherwise normal people. And although it shouldn't be an excuse, oftentimes it was the reason for my emotional outbursts and less than desired amount of patience. I tried to nip it in the bud as soon as I realized what I needed. It's difficult to do, but especially important if you have older kids, as they will be feeling the brunt of your outbursts.

△ *"All I wanted to do was throw the thing across the room, and hit it against the wall!" And no, I was not referring to a kid.*

What I needed was always the same. I needed to start exercising more, I needed more sleep, I needed a few minutes for me, and I needed to start adding something to my supplemental routine that would help regulate my hormones. I postponed taking an antidepressant, and I tried adding vitamin D to my diet. I also tried the herbal supplement St. John's Wart, at the advice of my doctor. Knowing that Joe was our last baby, I felt reassured that my hormones would finally have a chance to settle down and get back to normal. I knew this wasn't going to happen until my body stopped producing milk, and the supplements helped a little. It's difficult to say how effective they were, because life only got faster, busier, and scarier as our kids got older. As Joe approached his second birthday, I felt okay but not myself.

Six months after Joe was born, we had a lot of added stress in our lives for a number of reasons. We had all been home for summer, which meant more fighting, more messes, and stuck inside because of the scorching heat. Jesse's seizures had started a month earlier, and his feeding therapy was getting more challenging, for him and for me. And, sadly, my extended family was in the middle of a nightmare as our uncle was on trial for the murder of his wife (my aunt). The horror of the accident, and unbelievable accusation was beyond comprehension. We were devastated! With this going on, and the long list of weekly activities, I was surviving, but I decided I needed to start back on an antidepressant. It was what was best for our family and it really helped me get through an extremely tough time in our lives. I really started to feel like myself and I actually looked forward to working out and getting active again.

For the new moms who are able to stay home, be very careful not to let depression and loneliness creep up. It can be very subtle but serious. It is crucial that you get out and connect with other moms, both with and without your kids. Moms that stay home for an extended period of time after having a baby are very susceptible to having mood swings and experiencing depressing moments, sometimes several throughout the day.

> "My last and youngest daughter of four was a very hard baby. She had colic and reflux and cried non-stop. I never slept and was feeling so lost. I remember wishing I could just run away. It was like nothing I had ever felt and it scared me. I didn't want to tell anyone because I felt like such a bad mom. I finally opened up to someone close and she helped me realize I was experiencing postpartum depression. It is real and I'm lucky I had the support."
>
> — Wendy, veteran mother of 4

I remember this vividly in my experience as a first-time mom. I stayed home, not even getting out for groceries, mostly because I wasn't ready to leave the house. After the six-week recommended recovery, I left the house only for necessities. Over time, this desire for isolation grew and I started feeling worthless to the outside world, and very alone, which only made my depression worse. When I immersed myself with other activities and responsibilities, after Ryanne and Reese were older, my confidence and feeling of worth started to come back. I went back to school to pursue a teaching credential, and although difficult to do with two young children, I believe it saved me from falling deeper into isolation. Making and keeping connections with the outside world MUST be a part of your life as a mom, even if you have to go looking for it!

There are several factors that can contribute to postpartum depression. Initially, the baby blues happen from a lack of the hormones estrogen and progesterone. A continued feeling of depression after the initial period, or baby blues stage, may be related to a medical condition, which is another good reason to talk with your doctor. My doctor and others told me that a deficiency in vitamin D has been known to cause mood swings. An added supplement of vitamin D may help with this, but of course discuss everything with your doctor first, especially if you are breastfeeding. Herbal supplements can be helpful, and there are many. I can recommend one with confidence because it is natural and safe, and I've experienced amazing results with myself and with my kids. It is a Nrf2 activator and it is called Protandim. My experience with this all-natural activator was so life-changing I became involved with the company so that I could share my experience and distribute the product. But, again, research the benefits and the risks of everything first, and discuss it with your doctor. However, in saying this, please remember that doctors don't know about everything, and your own research, if done thoroughly, can be enough.

It's never easy to talk about something that causes shame or embarrassment. No mother wants to feel as if she doesn't love her baby or her children, let alone talk about it. This feeling is coming, in some form for most moms, so reach out to your network of family and friends to help you through it. Communication can get you through anything, so remember, talk about it! And please know that you are normal for needing this support—even if it feels like your needs are much larger than others.

△ *Making and keeping connections with the outside world MUST be a part of your life as a mom, even if you have to go looking for it!*

△ Notes

Four

Feeding: By Breast and Beyond

Another hot topic for the new mom is feeding your baby. It starts within minutes of giving birth. You hear your child for the first time, and although in the moment you won't think about it, you have probably thought about it for the past nine months, or longer. Will I breastfeed, or will I feed my baby formula? Now of course there are arguments for both but you will see that breastfeeding was always my first choice. And I ask that you at least consider it to be yours.

As is evident above, I am a total advocate of nursing, and for me, this was a no-brainer. I always knew I wanted to breastfeed. If you are choosing not to breastfeed, reading this section might not help you all that much, but please continue reading. I hope you will be more willing to give it a try. If you're on the fence, hopefully what you read in my experiences won't deter you from it. Although it was a rough start for me, I am so thankful I was able to continue with it, and I urge you to at least give it a try. It's much better and easier in so many ways. Take it one day at a time. Some nursing is better than no nursing, even if it's only for a month. If you are unable for medical reasons, or your body has difficulty producing enough milk, at least you tried your best. Don't beat yourself up about it. Sometimes it just doesn't work.

When my Ryanne was born I was nervous and worried about a lot of things. Will she latch on? Will I know if she's eating?

Reasons to think about breastfeeding first:

△   It's healthier.

△   It builds a strong immunity to disease and infection, especially early.

△   It creates an incomparable bond/connection.

△   It's cheaper than formula because it's FREE!

△   It helps you lose your baby weight. Your body can burn up to 500 calories per day producing milk.

△   It helps the uterus shrink to its normal size after birth, which can help with bleeding.

△   It's MUCH more convenient (can't accidentally leave your breasts can you!).

△   Breasts are larger than normal, which might be important to some. I know the dads don't mind.

△   No periods (sometimes for up to a year!) if you're nursing exclusively. Sadly, this doesn't happen for all nursing moms.

△   It's a fairly reliable form of birth control while nursing exclusively (in the first few months).

△   It's been linked to reducing your risk of developing breast cancer.

△   *The first time was quite pleasant, and it really did help me to connect with her. In the moment, having a baby is all so surreal and hard to grasp, but nursing made it real, and I began to feel like she was really mine.*

Will it hurt? We read and hear about so many different issues related to breastfeeding. I couldn't help but expect the worst of all I had heard. Thankfully, within two hours I was nursing, and doing it pretty well, and correctly. It didn't hurt at all and it was an amazing feeling. Although it was a little awkward at first, after seeing how comforting it was for her, I became very comfortable. But this changed quickly.

The first time was quite pleasant, and it really did help me to connect with her. In the moment, having a baby is all so surreal and hard to grasp. Nursing made it real and I began to feel like she was really mine. Of course, I wish I could say that it was always wonderful, easy, natural, no problem—but it was not! I realize that some breastfeeding moms don't have a lot of problems with sore nipples, infections, incorrect latch on,

Reasons for formula:

△ There's too much pain/difficulty breastfeeding.

△ Breasts are for sex, not feeding (a stigma both men and women can struggle with).

△ Breasts will age more gracefully if they aren't sucked on (one can hope, although not what really happens. They still lose their "grace.")

△ Easier for working moms. I completely agree with this, but are you working to pay for the formula?

△ It's easier to take trips away from baby.

△ Baby may need it for more calories (my little Jess man needed this).

△ Breastfeeding can be a sticky, smelly mess. But in my opinion, formula, formula poops, and formula spit-up smell much worse than breastmilk induced responses.

and the other difficulties that come with the initial stages of breastfeeding, but I sure did! I know a lot of moms who, like me, were not ready for it. I'll admit, I was warned about the sore, cracked, and bleeding nipples, but I was not expecting what I got!

After two or three feedings, I began to get sore. I checked for correct latch on, because what experts or consultants tell you is that it should not hurt or feel sore if the baby is latching on correctly. Maybe they don't say this any more, but this is what they used to say. In all my experiences, a correctly latched-on baby can still suck you dry! And this is literally what happens. If you think about it, how often does someone suck on your nipples? Well, answers may vary on this one. But it makes sense that your nipples are not used to the extra moisture, sucking, pulling, and biting, and they might get a little worn out. Correct or not, it still hurts! She was latching on correctly. Her wet diapers and satisfied state, my empty breasts, and her whole jaw sucking motion verified this. With each feeding it was getting more and more painful and uncomfortable. This is one detail of early motherhood my own mother never forgot! No doubt this is why she remembered to warn me.

△ *It makes sense that your nipples are not used to the extra moisture, sucking, pulling, biting, and they might get a little worn out. Correct or not, it still hurts! And she was latching on correctly.*

What can add to the discomfort is the reality that you don't have any milk yet, and the baby just sucks and sucks only getting very small amounts of colostrum—the thick, nutrient rich, antibody filled first milk. When nothing is coming out and you know it, it's frustrating, painful, and to be honest, completely miserable. For many moms, they endure this dry sucking for four to five days, and sometimes longer. My milk came in after only a few days, which helped. Some mothers wait for five to six days before they can feed their babies breast milk. Nursing within an hour or two of birth and nursing often will speed up milk production, which is a good thing. But it will also speed the development of the cracking and bleeding, which is what happened to me.

△ *My breasts were engorged and uncomfortably full of milk! My cup size grew by three letters!*

"My daughter had what's called a lip and tongue tie, making it difficult for her to latch deeply. This caused extreme pain that lasted much longer than what I heard was typical. After having this repaired, it got much better."

— Mama CC, new mom

By feeding number five my nipples were dry, cracked, and bleeding. I began to dread feeding time because it had gotten so bad. But I kept going. In case you are wondering, it is okay to keep nursing when your nipples are bleeding. In fact, you must continue to nurse or you may risk losing the ability to nurse at all. However, pumping is sometimes better if you are bleeding a lot and it can be less painful.

By the time I was home, I was cringing every time she latched on, sometimes with a few tears—and I'm not one to cry easily from pain. To make matters worse, I became extremely engorged, which means uncomfortably full of milk. I am not kidding! My cup size grew by three letters! I was lucky. And I do mean lucky in the sarcastic, what other painful problem am I going to get, sense of the word, because my milk supply came in after only two days. The typical four or five days would have allowed me time to adjust to the other discomforts I was experiencing, but I got them all at once. With extremely sore nipples, awful engorgement, and flu-like symptoms, (from engorgement and an oncoming infection), things were pretty miserable in the first few days. It did get much better, but not overnight.

Preventing and Addressing Sore Nipples

I was told about a few tricks that have been known to help with sore, cracked nipples. One is to use Lanolin and to rub it on two to three times a day during your last few months of pregnancy. This is more of a prevention tactic and it helps "prepare" your nipples for their upcoming battles. You can also use a washcloth and scrub your nipples to toughen them up. Still today, the thought of this makes me shutter. Scrub my nipples, no way! If this is for you, don't use soap because this will dry them out. Think mangle and moisturize. It might be too late to try this trick, but if not, do it! You may be much more comfortable in the first few days of nursing. The Lanolin can also be applied before and after each feeding. It won't hurt Baby, so it doesn't need to be washed off before feeding, and it can protect your nipples from moisture, similar to protecting a baby's bottom with cream or ointment. An easy, inexpensive tip that can help moisturize and heal sensitive and cracked nipples is to rub breastmilk on sore nipples after feeding, and allow them to air-dry.

△ **TIP:** *Rubbing breastmilk on nipples after feeding can help moisturize and heal cracked and sore nipples.*

One of the best products ever made for easing nipple pain, and also for keeping moms breastfeeding, is the nipple shield. The shield saved me. I was ready to give up because nursing had become so painful, but when I started using the nipple shield the pain was gone (I know it sounds like a commercial). It protects the nipple, and sometimes even helps babies to latch on properly if they are struggling. It especially helped Jesse to latch. He struggled with sucking, and many other things in the early stages, but the shield helped him and me in many ways. Although the shield was NOT recommended by nurses or lactation consultants, during my breastfeeding days, I listen to my instinct and chose to use it anyway. I had success using the shield with all my babies, and it kept me nursing.

△ **TIP:** *Try the nipple shield for relief. It eases the pain and can help babies latch on in the early days postpartum.*

Many of my mommy friends were discouraged from using the shield, or anything that would potentially confuse the baby's feeding experience. One friend in particular, had a baby who preferred only one breast. This friend fulfilled her baby's desire and only breastfed on the favorite side. In addition to this she was discouraged from using the nipple shield to help with her sore nipple. She never used it, and ended up with severe mastitis on the non-preferred breast, and a nipple that was hanging literally by a thread. Her preferred breast and nipple had been mangled to pieces. I apologize for the graphic details, but can you imagine? I cringe every time I think about it.

> "The nipple shield helped so much to allow my nipples to heal, which was a lifesaver! I was surprised when I asked the lactation consultant about the nipple shields and she told me that they do not recommend them, but she didn't really tell me why."
>
> — Michelle J, mother of 2

In addition, she had to stop nursing to allow her nipple to heal, which forced her baby to breastfeed on a side he did not like and had resisted for so long. This was not a happy time for her. In her opinion, and I agree, if she had been more confident and informed about her options before having these issues, she would have used the nipple shield and insisted that her baby nurse on BOTH sides. The nipple shield would have prevented both of the problems she had in the beginning. If you need it, use it!

As wonderful as it is, there is a downside to using the shield. It's easy to become dependent on using the nipple shield, which can and will make nursing tougher in the long run. For example, the shield, like bottles (if you go that route), will need to be washed after every use, which can be a pain when you're feeding every two hours. It also needs to be packed with the diaper bag if you decide to go anywhere with your baby, which is likely. Adding to your list of things to pack is not always the easiest and most convenient when you're a new mommy. One of the luxuries of breastfeeding is that you don't have to pack anything, or worry about forgetting anything for feeding. Wean your baby from the shield as soon as you think you and your baby are ready. I used the shield for about two weeks with all five of my babies. By that time they were latching on well and eating well, and I was tired of washing it ten times a day. Plus, my nipples were tough and I didn't need it any more. I usually weaned them from it slowly, taking it from one side first and then gradually eliminating it completely within a day or two.

Other Unpleasants

A few other unpleasant breastfeeding struggles that I had the pleasure of experiencing were thrush and mastitis. Unfortunately, I had both with my first four kids. For some reason, I didn't notice anything major with Joe, the baby.

Thrush

Thrush is an infection caused from growing bacteria in a moist environment. This is an infection the baby gets. It's basically a yeast infection in the mouth. It looks like little white spots on the tongue or inside of the mouth. Sometimes the white spots don't show up, or aren't easily noticed, until the pain starts. It doesn't hurt the baby but it can be very unpleasant for the mother.

△ *The main symptom I remember from a thrush infection was a prickly sensation in the nipple. It felt like needles poking directly into my nipple, right at latch on.*

The main symptom I remember from this infection was a prickly sensation in the nipple. It felt like needles poking directly into the nipple and it can get worse and be extremely painful if left untreated. You can usually expect a prescription for the baby (mouth drops likely four times a day), and instructions to rub the liquid on your nipples after every feeding followed by air drying. If you're like me, you might laugh at the thought of sitting, exposed while giving your nipples some air. Not only because the visual makes me laugh, but also because I rarely had time to sit and do nothing. The doctor prescribed oral Nystatin. This medication is perfect for nursing because it is safe for baby and you won't need to wash your nipples before feeding. The topical Nystatin isn't as convenient or helpful because it means you have to keep track of one more medication, and it also has to be washed off before nursing. If given a choice, and you generally are, I would ask for the oral Nystatin drops for both you and your baby, or a similar medication that might become more commonly used.

Mastitis

△ **FYI:** *Mastitis is an infection that can cause flulike symptoms and localized soreness in the breast. If not discovered and tended to early, it will require antibiotics.*

Mastitis can be a little more serious for the mother, but it doesn't affect the baby. This situation usually develops from breast engorgement and can be very uncomfortable and serious. Mastitis is generally caused from a plugged milk duct and can cause a number of painful symptoms, such as redness and hard, large lumps that are extremely sore to the touch. You may also start to feel achy, which is a definite sign that you are getting an infection and you will want to call your doctor right away. You will likely need a prescription to help resolve it.

> "I was not warned about Mastitis, and the pain it could cause. I also didn't know I could prevent it from happening. This would have been useful information."
>
> — Mama T, new mom

This particular infection comes on very quickly, too. At least it did for me. It's important to pay attention to your body and notice changes right away. If you feel soreness in your breast, it may take only a few hours for the pain to become extreme, and the achy feelings to take over your entire body. The tenderness and sensitivity to touch can get so bad it could bring you to tears. By this time, you will feel aches all over, and the only thing you can think about is going to bed. If it progresses to this point, it will be difficult to shake the infection and massage the pain away. Nursing will hurt *in* your nipple, as well as in the tender area. Breastfeed and massage the area as much as you can stand and this will help tremendously. If you stay ahead of it, the soreness will go away within a day or two. If you find yourself feeling worse, and have a fever, you will need to see a doctor for antibiotics.

A few ways to help reduce the pain associated with mastitis and even avoid the need for a prescription are to nurse often while massaging the tender area. This might be really tough and painful, but it does help, and it's the best way to ward off an oncoming infection. I never had to take an antibiotic for mastitis and if you can identify the signs early and are aware of the infection, you won't need antibiotics.

Another trick you can try is cabbage. Several friends of mine swore by this, and even my midwife recommended it to me. I tried it with my first baby, but unfortunately can't remember if it worked. Unless you have cabbage on hand, or can send your husband or a friend out to get some, this tip might not be terribly convenient, but it's still worth a try! Take a generous-sized leaf of cabbage, and place it against your skin at the tender site. It may help with the inflammation and pain. Continue nursing and massaging the area to stimulate the flow of breast milk from the plugged duct. If you've defeated the infection on your own, you should feel much better the next day, and normal by two days post infection.

> "When I got Mastitis, I was taking Ibuprofen 4–6 hours around the clock, to help with the pain. When the Ibuprofen wore off that first evening, I was in so much pain, and had a fever and chills. I was so exhausted, that my husband had to help me get from the bed to the shower. Standing in the hot shower was the only thing that made it feel better."
>
> — Mama C, new mom

Mastitis can become so severe, that not only can you get extremely sick, but the plugged milk duct can also become a lump that never goes away. A friend of mine shared her first breastfeeding experience with me, and it deserves some attention. Fourteen years after breastfeeding her first child, a large lump in her breast remains, from the severe Mastitis infection she experienced. Her experience could have been avoided had she been told about possible difficulties and infections, as well as prevention and treatments.

△ *Breastfeeding may seem foreign and uncomfortable for a few weeks, but after two to three weeks of breastfeeding, you will begin to feel like a pro and it will start to seem so easy. After about six weeks it will feel as if you've been nursing for years.*

Breastfeeding may seem foreign and uncomfortable at first, but after two to three weeks, you will begin to feel like a pro and it will start to seem so easy. After about six weeks it will feel as if you've been nursing for years. Your supply will be better regulated and you should feel more comfortable. You will notice the fluctuations in your breast size and fullness. You will feel more full in the morning, especially if you've stopped breastfeeding during the night. This is a great time to use your breast pump to get a little extra breast milk to store. Throughout the day you will go from full to not-so-full. Your breasts will tell you a lot about when your baby needs to eat, and how much he's eating. They will also tell you if he's not eating enough. If, at the end of a day you start feeling empty, or you feel full after each feeding, it might be a sign that your baby isn't eating enough. Let your breasts "speak" to you and pay attention to what they are saying. Maybe your husband can have this job. I'm sure he wouldn't mind.

"I thought breastfeeding was going to be a totally natural and easy experience. For me, it was pretty much everything BUT that! It was painful from the beginning, but after a few weeks it got much better."

— Mama K, new mom

Once you've figured out the art of breastfeeding, taking care of your baby will get even more exciting! You may even be ready to try it in public! Just be sure to pack your nursing cover or blanket. It takes a little longer than six weeks to perfect the act of discreet nursing without a cover. But you'll get there. So, stick with it! You will be so glad you did, and so will your baby.

Cesarean

If you happened to have a cesarean, like my sister, then breastfeeding and recovery will be a little more difficult and take a little longer. The baby will need to be in a specific position, usually the "football hold," which is to the side instead of in front. The nurses will help you with this. You will need to avoid having the baby on the sore area. A Boppy pillow or similar 'C' shaped pillow can be a lifesaver for breastfeeding after a cesarean, as it protects the belly from pressure. I never delivered by cesarean but my sister did, twice. She shared her experience with me.

Breastfeeding Essentials

You will want a lot of rags! Don't get sucked in by the thin, pretty, colorful rags, which aren't absorbent and will leave you with a soaked rag and a wet shirt. I recommend the bulk packs of white cloth diapers found at stores like Target or Walmart. They are definitely not pretty, but they are better! If you want pretty, find some creative ideas and customize the white cloths to your liking. Thick, terry cloth or cotton are surprisingly good at soaking up milk, spit-up, or whatever.

△ *FYI: The boppy pillow can protect the belly from pressure after having a cesarean.*

If you even *think* you *might* breastfeed in public or around others (and whether you plan to or not, you most definitely will), have a nursing shawl or cover on hand. You can find these online and in most stores with a baby department. A large muslin blanket works well too, but it requires some skill. The cover eliminates the worry that you will be exposed if baby pulls on it.

Having a lot of nursing pads will save you, your clothing, and your self-esteem. If you leak breast milk and do not have a barrier layer between your bra and clothing, you will end up with two wet circles on your shirt. This is more likely to happen in the beginning, when you don't have a feeding routine yet, but it *can* happen when you don't expect it to. This can be embarrassing. There are both disposable and reusable pads, depending on your preference. Changing them often will help with leaks, and also help prevent infection.

A bottle warmer (for frozen or cold breast milk) is important although not necessary. A cup and warm running water works just as well to warm breast milk, although it might not be as quick as a warmer. On the up side, it takes up less space and is cheaper, if you can manage without it.

Breastfeeding Essentials

As moms of the 21st century we are very lucky to have access to the latest "must-have" products. But we also must filter through a lot of the unnecessary stuff. Here are a few items I consider must-haves for breastfeeding or baby feeding in general:

△ A lot of burp rags!

△ A nursing shawl or cover

△ Lots of nursing pads

△ Bottle warmer

△ Breastmilk storage bags

△ A GOOD breast pump

△ Hands-free pumping bra

△ Comfortable and flattering nursing bras

△ A nursing camisole

△ The Nipple Shield

Breast milk storage bags or bottles are a necessity. I preferred the bags because they thawed faster and were easier to use. Good-quality bags will protect frozen milk and won't break or tear. Spend the extra cash if you can. Breast milk is very valuable and you don't want to lose any milk to a leaky bag.

It is highly likely that you will need a breast pump (a double electric pump if you will be working). I recommend Medela and Playtex brand pumps. Although expensive, they will save you from interruptions in your nursing and pumping schedule. Pumping can be frustrating at times, even more so if your pump isn't working efficiently. I can't say enough about having a good breast pump. It really is priceless. I had the-top-of-the-line Medela breast pump, and I was able to breastfeed for almost a year, while working full time.

△ *I will admit that I pumped while I commuted to work. This might be considered distracted driving, but as long as you set up before you start driving, and clean up after you've stopped, it's pretty safe.*

Along with a good double breast pump, you'll want a hands free pumping bra which will allow you to be productive while you pump. I will admit that I pumped while commuting to work. This might be considered distracted driving, but as long as you set up before you start driving, and clean up after you've stopped, it's pretty safe. But I'd advise you to drive the speed limit. It might be slightly embarrassing explaining the situation to a police officer if you get pulled over for speeding. Ha!

My one complaint about breastfeeding is that it can be tough to find a comfortable, yet flattering nursing bra—especially if you are more endowed than a pre-baby A or B cup size. Having several comfortable bras is key. Don't be afraid to spend a little extra money for support, comfort, and a flattering fit. You have a new figure, and it can be a struggle to find something that enhances the good stuff and hides the other stuff. So try *several* different styles and brands because a good, supportive and flattering bra will really boost your confidence and make you feel good. If you've got smaller breasts, a nursing camisole is great, and I've heard very comfortable. I don't have, and never did have, little boobs, so this was never an option for me.

If you haven't guessed, I am a strong advocate of nursing, and I have included more useful information for nursing moms throughout the book. For those of you who have chosen the alternative, I really urge you to give nursing a try. Take it one day at a time, and you may find it much better and easier than expected. Any amount of breastfeeding is better than none. I do understand, however, that medical conditions prevent many mothers from breastfeeding. It may be that a health condition of the mother is making it difficult to breastfeed, or has removed it as an option altogether. It is also possible the baby is struggling.

My son Jesse had health issues early on, the biggest being his struggle to gain weight. With his swallowing disorder, problems with constipation, and undiagnosed kidney issues, he never wanted to eat. Eventually, I had to stop nursing and give him formula with extra calories. He was only four months old. I was very disappointed, but I did what was necessary for the health of my child. And, if nursing is not for you, for whatever reason, formula is a very healthy alternative.

The time it takes, the condition of your breasts after breastfeeding, and how much your baby is eating will determine when the next feeding will likely be needed. If your baby breastfeeds for ten to fifteen minutes total, and one or both of your breasts feel as if they have been emptied, your baby will likely not need to eat again until two or three hours later.

ADVICE FOR FIRST-TIME BREASTFEEDING

Step-by-step instructions

△   Get comfortable in whatever position you choose to use or try. Try different positions to find what works best for you. The cradle position (baby's head in bend of elbow with Baby across the stomach), was best for me and my babies and was the most comfortable. It's also the most discreet way to breastfeed in public.

△   Position baby close with his mouth level with your nipple, and head tilted slightly up. The cradle hold allows you to adjust Baby's head, body, or mouth position.

△   Use your nipple as a trigger for your baby to open. Rub your nipple on his bottom lip.

△   Hold your breast with the nipple facing Baby's mouth and flatten it so it looks like you are about to feed your baby a sandwich. Can you visualize it?

△   Use force! This is where new moms are timid when they shouldn't be. When your baby's mouth is at its widest, shove baby gently towards you and the nipple. You really do need to be quick and somewhat forceful with baby's head to your breast. Push his head and hold it into your breast, making sure to keep his nose clear (you can use your thumb or finger to pull your breast away from his nose).

△   With correct latch-on, you will see a very wide open-mouth, the whole areola covered, and you will notice an up-and-down movement of the jaw (whole jaw sucking) where the jaw meets the earlobe.

△   The first few times should be painless, with correct latch on, but after this your nipples may begin to get sore. Soreness early on can also be from incorrect latch on, so pay attention to the jaw movement of your baby. Remember the nipple shield, and verify with your nurse that your baby is latching on correctly. All babies feed differently. Some may be very efficient, and only need and want five to ten minutes at a time. If your breasts feel like they've been emptied, and your baby is having wet diapers, he's probably getting enough. If your breasts still feel very full, or feel as if they haven't changed much, this is something to note and watch. Some babies may take longer to eat. It's likely they just enjoy the experience as much as the milk, and they want to take their time; however, don't allow him too much time, as this will create an unnecessary habit.

Signs of Early Feeding Struggles

Our little angel Jesse took a very long time to nurse, but my breasts never felt empty. They always felt full. He also never spit up, which is something that my other four did frequently after feeding. I don't remember needing or using a burp rag with Jesse. I don't think I even included them in his diaper bag, which completely threw me off when Joe was born. No spit up was a sign that something wasn't quite right. But it was a very subtle thing, and I just thought his feeding was different from his siblings, and not necessarily a problem; however, when he wasn't gaining weight like my other kids, but was taking twenty to thirty minutes to eat, we started to wonder if he was having difficulty feeding. Did he have a weak suck, or was he having trouble swallowing? Maybe he was extra tired so he wasn't very efficient at eating. I went through everything I could think of, based on my experiences with my other children. What I did not think about was that he might have a neurological problem that made it difficult to eat. Why would I?

After discovering other issues related to a neurological delay, we wondered if his feeding was related to this issue. I was convinced he had some sort of swallowing problem and I was worried it hurt to swallow, or he was having difficulty. I voiced my concerns with the pediatrician, and finally, after a year of very slow weight gain, and developmental delays, we had a swallow study done at Stanford Medical Center. Appointments with specialized doctors are not easy to get, and they take many weeks, sometimes months to happen.

The diagnostic results of his study were that he had insufficient tongue movement when drinking from a bottle, and that he had difficulty swallowing (pharyngeal dysphagia). Wow! This explained a lot, and helped us to understand why he had such a noticeable gag reflex. We adjusted our feeding methods, and saw some improvement. For example, we fed him upright, allowing gravity to work with him, and used different nipple tips. The moral of this story—pay attention to how your breasts feel before and after feeding, and also take note of wet diapers, and spit up! These situations should exist and if they don't, you'll want to find out why.

△ *If you are concerned about something because you feel it, tell your doctor. Be persistent! They don't always take your concerns seriously, but your instincts are so much stronger than you may realize.*

△ *I felt guilty that I had to stop giving him breast milk. But as I've said before, a little breastfeeding is better than no breastfeeding, and he is a very smart, happy, and healthy kid*

The other thing to take away from our experience with little Jesse is that you, the mother, understand your baby better than anyone. If you are concerned about something because you feel it, tell your doctor. Be persistent! Doctors don't always take your concerns seriously, but your instincts are so much stronger than you may realize. You see your child every day. This is worth much more than the opinion of a medical doctor, especially considering that doctors see them for only a few short minutes at each appointment, with weeks or even months in between.

When Jesse was three years old we took him to a follow-up appointment with his neurologist. One of the best in the state, and a little egotistical, he was certain Jesse had Williams syndrome. He nearly diagnosed him before we left the room. He made this diagnosis in five minutes based on his head shape and facial features. I, of course, completely disagreed! I knew Jesse and argued that he looked just like his siblings with their TV heads and button noses! He said to me, "I hope you're right, but I don't think so," and gave me the order for the blood test. Four months later, we're in his office again listening to him tell us he was wrong. Jesse did not have Williams Syndrome just as I thought! Trust what you know about your child and put up a fight if you need to!

Advice for First-Time Pumping

First of all, you *will* need a breast pump, even if you don't intend on returning to work. Although expensive, it will be worth it. It will be especially important in the first few days post delivery. Most nurses and lactation consultants will tell you not to pump when your milk comes in. I believe this is to avoid producing more milk than you need. It makes sense not to confuse your body's supply-and-demand radars by pumping, however, sometimes it's the only thing that will give you comfort. If you will be returning to work in six, eight or twelve weeks, you will want to have a supply of milk handy for introducing a bottle, or for a night out with your mate; it's a good idea to pump in the few weeks before you go back to work. Now, I'm not a lactation consultant, but I do believe that nursing five babies entitles me to a little respect when I offer breastfeeding advice.

When babies are very little, it can be difficult to get them to eat when you want or need them to. By introducing a bottle early, this dilemma can be solved with a ready-to-go bottle. When you are facing a time constraint and getting ready for an outing, it's likely Baby won't be on your schedule. If he is ready for a feeding, but won't wake up to eat before departure, you may be facing a late arrival to work or an appointment. You might try pumping and taking a ready-to-go bottle. If you have a good quality-pump, this strategy will be much faster than nursing, and you can feed baby as soon as you arrive at your appointment. Most likely, your baby will stay asleep when you transfer him to his car seat and you will have a bottle to feed him when you arrive. Another bonus is that you won't have to breastfeed in a public place, which is sometimes a hassle you don't want to face.

This idea did not come to me until I had Joe. Prior to having Joe I had breastfed four kids before him and had been stressed out and been late so many times. Knowing they would be hungry, I often waited for them to wake on their own so I could feed them before leaving. As a last resort and at the last minute I would try to wake them only to have them fall back to sleep without eating. It was a daily struggle. In my mind, feeding him right before leaving would allow me to avoid doing it while I was out on errands or during an appointment. Sounds logical, right? This strategy, however, involved waking him thirty minutes before leaving, to allow time for the whole process of breastfeeding—both breasts, burping, and a diaper change. Waking a sleeping baby is rarely easy, and goes against the cardinal rule of caring for babies that states to never wake a sleeping baby. Plus, often times he had only been asleep for a short period of time. Waking him was hard.

Before I got smart—duh—I spent hours and precious energy worrying about these scenarios. Not wanting to wake them (or unable to really wake them), I would wait as long as possible, finally get them up, feed them on one breast (which is a mediocre job, but all I would have time for) and then put them in the car hoping they would fall back to sleep. What I finally

△ **TIP:** *When baby is sleeping, ready to feed, and you are trying to leave the house, prepare a ready-to-go bottle. Pump a bottle rather than breastfeed to save time and the need to wake Baby before leaving.*

realized-ta-da!- is that I could pump enough in ten minutes for a full feeding, and feed them when they woke up any time, any place with ease. This situation was a lot more predictable, and on my timeline and not Baby's. Boy was this helpful! I wish I had thought of this sooner.

> **"No one told me that when your milk comes in you experience a lot of weird symptoms. I got super hot and nervous for no reason."**
>
> — Mama M, mother of 2

When your milk comes in, boy does it come in! My first time milk came in at day two, in the middle of the night. I woke up early in the morning on day three in a pool of breast milk. I was drenched, hair and all! My bed was soaked through to the mattress, and I was thinking, "How disgusting!" This was not what I expected at all. NO ONE warned me about this! As the day went on, my breasts got larger and larger, and firmer by the minute. Eventually, they were so full of milk that they felt and looked like basketballs! No joke! The only option I had was to pump to relieve some pressure, and soften my breasts enough so that my baby could latch. When breasts get too firm, it's very difficult for Baby to latch successfully. My advice is, *yes, pump*! It won't hurt anything, and it will give relief and allow for Baby to latch on more easily. Plus, you will have breast milk to store for the two-week bottle test run. You'll find more about this in the "Going Back to Work" chapter.

> **"I breastfed for the first six weeks—this was all I could do. It felt so boring and time consuming for me! I was feeding all the time and pumping as well, so others could feed him too. Our pediatrician suggested we try formula, and this was so much easier! I did feel a little guilt about stopping, but I think this was what was best for me."**
>
> — Mama K, new mom

One of my best friends was advised not to pump in the beginning. When her milk came in, she really did have basketballs! It was her first baby, so naturally she listened to the lactation consultant and did not pump. She was huge, uncomfortable, inexperienced—and miserable. She was so firm and full that her baby could not latch on to eat. Thankfully, I went to see her and encouraged her to pump. She pumped just enough from each side to relieve the pressure that was making things so difficult. Within ten minutes, her little Ella was breastfeeding, and my friend was smiling.

Formula Feeding

I am a strong believer in exclusive breastfeeding for as long as possible, although I wouldn't go as far as breastfeeding a two-year-old, because it's not for me. Many moms do continue breastfeeding beyond a year, and this is completely up to them and what works for them, and their beliefs. I also fed my babies formula. As I said earlier, Jesse had a swallowing disorder that prevented him from breastfeeding. He needed a prescription-strength, thicker formula to help him swallow, and gain weight. Unfortunately, breastfeeding was over when Jesse started on formula. He started on formula at four months old.

Jack also started on formula at four months. When I went back to work teaching, Jack was four months old, but I couldn't keep up my milk supply to breastfeed exclusively. My pump was mediocre, and my work schedule was very demanding. Once I went back to work I was only able to pump for a few months. When he was six months old, Jack started on formula during the day. He stayed on three bottles of formula during the day, and I breastfed at morning and at night for as long as possible. After a few months of this, when he was nine months old, it became too tough to breastfeed. I felt guilty that I had to stop giving him breast milk. But as I've said before, a little breastfeeding is better than no breastfeeding, and he is a very smart, happy and healthy kid. He is also kind, and very loving.

Information Only Veterans Know: Spit Up

Every baby is different. You will experience a lot of the same mishaps and victories with each one, but you may also get brand-new, crazy, and totally unique moments as well. For example, most babies spit up after eating. This is nothing new, even to the first-time mom. That's why the "burp rag" has become such a popular gift at baby showers. They are a necessity. All my babies were quite skilled in this category. They *always* spit up, and it was always A TON! If I had measured the amount of spit up I experienced daily I could easily claim that on a good day it was about two ounces with each feeding. A possible exaggeration, but it does seem like a whole lot when it happens.

For a time, Jack was the champion spitter. He seemed to spit up *everything* he ate. Then came Joe, who soaked through three to five burp rags a day. I couldn't wash the rags fast enough, and resorted to using a lot of dishtowels. It slowed as they got bigger and as my milk supply steadied. It's gross, I know, but gross is normal in motherhood. This is especially so on a full production day (near engorgement). Don't be alarmed if you have an Olympic spitter! As long as the spit-up remains whitish yellow and doesn't smell too much like vomit, it's normal.

Differentiating between real vomit smell and excess spit-up vomit smell can be difficult. The key is whether your baby is fussing and isn't his usual self. If it smells strongly like vomit, or your baby isn't eating normally or acting like himself, he might not be feeling well.

Bloody Spit-Up

When Jack was four months old, I noticed blood on his crib sheets. Of course, I panicked! I called the pediatrician right away. Apparently, it is possible for a baby to suck hard enough to draw blood from the nipple, even after the initial cracking and bleeding has healed. From a pediatrician's perspective, this is what likely happened. It wasn't a lot of blood, but any amount of blood is enough to freak you out! When you have children, surprises are lurking around every corner. There is this thing called a mother's instinct, however, and in the end go with your gut. Don't be afraid to be *that* new mom. *Those* moms have valid reason's for their actions, and I was self-conscious about calling too much, so I often hesitated. Peace of mind goes a long way.

Crying Before, During, or After Feeding

Another, very useful discovery for me in feeding my babies came when Jack was four months old. It was such an amazing revelation that as I mentioned earlier, it became my inspiration for this book. Although I experienced these very frustrating "episodes" with all my kids, it wasn't until Jack that I finally figured out the problem. Again, all babies are different, and the reasons for the crying fits during feedings may have come, or for you may come from other discomforts. I'm confident at some point you will experience it. Here's the scenario...

Jack was four months old. It had been four hours since he had eaten. I knew he was very hungry and getting increasingly upset. I got home, so excited to be with him and to be the only person who could give him what he needed. I sat down and started nursing. He was so hungry that I could hear him gulping down fresh milk, and he seemed completely content. All of a sudden, he pulled away and cried out. I pulled him closer. He latched on and continued eating. After about ten seconds he did it again. He started to get upset and frustrated. I tried to remain calm, but I couldn't understand what the problem was. After about two or three minutes of "force feeding" him, I had nearly lost it and he was inconsolable. That feeling of failure and the wacky hormones started to creep up on me. I knew he was hungry and I couldn't understand why he wouldn't eat. He was extremely bothered and uninterested, or so it seemed.

So what was wrong? Well, it might have been that he had a tummy ache or was going through one of his "colic" moments (crying fits that can last for hours). This wasn't his typical behavior. Maybe he needed to burp. I knew that Jack often ate quickly and forcefully, especially when he was very hungry. I was confident he was getting food, but I never thought

△ *I noticed, especially when he was very hungry, that Jack would eat quickly and forcefully. I knew he was getting food, but I never thought about the air he might have been swallowing.*

about the air he might have been swallowing during the process. I'm sure you can imagine how you feel when you have air somewhere that needs to come out! It wasn't until Jack that I really realized this discomfort. It was very frustrating because I knew he was hungry, but he wouldn't stay latched on and he was crying a lot.

When I finally noticed these moments with Jack, I would burp him. Sometimes it took five or ten minutes to get that burp. Hearing an adult-quality burp come out of my little baby's mouth made me laugh. But soon I realized what a talented little boy I had! He was a spitter and an exceptional burper! While this made me proud—ha!—I felt even better after discovering the reason for his crying fits. When Jack started crying or screaming out during feeding, I stopped, walked, and burped him. With the air out, he felt perfectly fine and ready to eat again.

Because Jack was unusually gassy, I adjusted my normal nursing patterns to try to alleviate or lessen the problem. My babies were all efficient eaters, and typically ate for five to ten minutes per side. Yours may take longer if he dawdles or is easily distracted. Jack would eat for five to ten minutes on each side, but then I began stopping after every two to three minutes to burp him. Amazingly, this helped with the amount of air he took in, and it also helped reduce how much he was spitting up. I imagine the amount of milk he was spitting up was related to his gassiness and the air he was swallowing. It might be something to try. In my experience, the more often you burp them, the more comfortable they will be.

After realizing this, I was able to alter the feeding situations for Jack, and did the same thing for the other two boys. They too were gassy (like most babies) and needed constant burping. Like Jack, they would pull away from the bottle and breast after an ounce, and become uninterested in eating. This lack of gas worried me with Jesse because he had always struggled with eating and weight gain. But with Joe, I knew the gas was "in the air." Search and destroy was my motto. So I did everything I could to find the air and get it out! Once the air was out, (and the spit-up) the feeding continued peacefully.

The fussy moments related to gas aren't always isolated to feedings. It can happen at any time, so it doesn't hurt to assume you *might* be able to help when they have these moments. Try to burp him first by walking, patting, and bouncing. Holding him high on your shoulder can sometimes help push the air out. If it doesn't happen, your baby might just be having his fussy time, and that's okay, too.

A frequent misconception that new moms, and sometimes even veteran moms have is the need to feed with every whimper from her baby. A crying baby doesn't always mean a hungry one. This is one of the most common assumptions that new moms make. This can result in overfeeding. I believe this is why many first born babies are *really* healthy.

Our daughter Ryanne was a very chubby baby who loved to eat. My initial instinct was to feed her any time she cried. Thankfully my mother helped me realize this was unnecessary and likely not the only reason she got upset. So, I focused on diagnosing the problem instead of assuming she was always hungry. I've seen this reaction with almost every mom I know, especially in the first weeks after delivery and during nighttime feedings. It can be very difficult to pass up an opportunity to calm a crying baby with milk, however, an amazing milk supply and a big appetite equal the perfect recipe for overeating and overflow. This won't hurt Baby but it will produce a lot more spit up and a baby that is used to eating on command. If your baby is getting enough every two to three hours this should be sufficient. It's unlikely he will need to eat more often. At night is no exception. However, you will notice fluctuations in appetite as your baby grows, so it's important to pay attention to these changes, as well.

The spit up, crying fits, and discomforts that most babies experience decrease significantly around four months. This is also when I started noticing less of the crying fits associated with colic. Life should get a little easier once their little tummies get used to the milk or formula. As they get older, they also take in less air when they eat, which reduces the need for frequent burping.

△ **FYI:** *A crying baby doesn't always mean a hungry one. Many moms make the mistake of feeding their babies the moment they make a sound. Think about the last feeding, when and how efficient it was, and allow this to determine the need to feed or not to feed.*

Feeding at Five to Six Months: Introducing Solids

Introducing solids is easy. Feeding them solids might not be. How they react to what they eat can be messy if you're not ready for it. This last little bit on feeding will be short and to the point, but it will include some useful and important nuggets.

△ **FYI:** *The first introduction to solids is very messy, so arm them with a heavy bib and relax! They may not eat a whole lot. Constipation is a potential result of introducing solids, as they are now eating more starches and thicker textures.*

In general, I introduced all of my babies to solids around five months old. Pediatricians and others might say that sooner is better. It really doesn't matter when as long as it's after four months, and sooner than six, unless otherwise directed by the pediatrician. I typically introduced one food at a time, and isolated the new food with familiar foods for a few days. In case of an allergy, it's easier to identify the culprit if you give only one new food at a time. I started with baby rice cereal, then oatmeal, whole grain cereal, and so on. Fruits and vegetables were introduced after the cereals, and usually once they hit six months. As I introduced each food and each meal, I maintained the same amount of breastmilk or formula throughout the day. Typically, I would give them the first "meal" an hour after their first morning bottle or breast. As I increased solid feedings to two times and three times each day, I tried to give the meals (two to four ounces of solids) an hour after their breastmilk or formula. This worked well for maintaining a regular eating schedule. I alternated breast milk and solids throughout the day. As they got older and more accustomed to eating a variety of foods, maintaining a schedule wasn't as important. But getting enough breastmilk and/or formula was important, so I paid attention to the schedule.

The first introduction to solids is very messy! They *will* spit it out, which is generally a reaction to the texture and the pushing movement of their tongue. Some just might not like it, so put a heavy-duty bib on them and relax. It's fun and entertaining, and they probably won't eat much. The first few days will be for the experience of the taste, texture of the food, and the movement of the tongue. You won't need to prepare a lot of food, and you'll want to use more water, as opposed to less. The transition will be easier if baby rice cereal is runny, and closer to what they are used to. If it's too thick, it might constipate them; however, they will likely get a little constipation with the introduction of solid food. Their little tummies need time to adjust. As long as you include the natural laxatives like prunes, apricots, and plums, every other day, it shouldn't be too tough on them. Apple juice also helps with constipation, but use sparingly. Try to avoid applesauce because it can constipate. Other constipating foods are dairy and starches, such as potatoes and rice.

If you find that your baby is grunting a lot, fussier than normal, and crying out in obvious discomfort, it may be that he is constipated. If he hasn't had a bowel movement in a few days, is new to solids, and is experiencing the above symptoms, it's very likely it's constipation. Give a few bites of prunes or apricots as soon as possible, and this should help. Too many prunes, however, will give you a big purple mess of poop!—so be careful.

This topic brings me to another very important point. When you give foods of different colors, you will find different colored poop in the diaper. Carrots turn baby poop red or orange. Beets in your diet or baby's can also affect color. Red is the most alarming color because it can look like blood in the stools. If you notice a change in your baby's poop, think about what he's eaten recently or whether he's been sick. This might help explain it, and hopefully avoid an unnecessary trip to the doctor.

Homemade Baby Food: It's Easy!

As you start introducing more solids, and different foods, you may notice how expensive it is to buy baby food. If you've ever tasted it, most of it isn't that good either. The fruits tend to be okay, and sweet potatoes are often a favorite. Anything with meat was never very appealing to my kids and had very little or no flavor. It was actually pretty gross. For many years I thought I was too busy to make my own baby food. So, for a long time I bought jars of baby food and spent a lot of money on food that didn't taste very good and wasn't as healthy as homemade.

△ *FYI: When you feed your baby carrots or sweet potatoes, don't be surprised to find orange or red poop in the diaper.*

When Jesse started on solids at age four, we had to feed him high calorie-foods like avocado, and we needed him to like what he was eating so I started making his baby food. It was then that I realized how easy it was, how much better it tasted, and how much money we were saving. The fact that it was all organic was also good and we knew exactly what he was eating. When he started refusing food, I slowed down on making the baby food, but continued to make some for Joe. Now that Jesse is eating pureed foods, we feed him ninety percent organic homemade purees. He eats twenty ounces of food a day, so you can imagine how much food I have to make. But it really is easy, and you can add so much flavor to everything. It's also much easier to hide foods like spinach and carrots. Here is a list of essentials for feeding solids to your baby, and for making your own baby food.

Baby Food Preparation Necessities

△ Short, flat, and shallow baby spoons (easy for baby and they won't tip the bowl over).

△ Short and wide feeding bowls (they don't tip over as easily and are also better to work with when self feeding begins).

△ Baby food freezing containers with lids and trays.

△ A really good blender.

△ A few baby food recipe books to help you get started.

△ Freezer bins for keeping frozen baby food organized.

△ Zip lock bags or ice cube trays for storing small amounts of frozen food.

△ A system for labeling bags and containers. (I use a Sharpie to write on the bags—nothing special.)

Feeding: A Picky Eater

At first introduction of solids, most babies aren't picky. They will eat most of what they are given. I introduced the vegetables first, because they don't taste quite as good as the fruits. As your little ones get older, they will form preferences for certain foods, and will love some and refuse others. Try not to allow them too much control in what they eat when they are little. It's not easy to force them to eat what they don't like, but a few bites of the yucky stuff will teach them a lot about eating, and about who is in control. I discuss this in detail in Jesse's feeding therapy chapter, as regaining control was the focus in the first few weeks of therapy. As they get older, they will start to test you at meal times. And after a few kids, and lots of advice from others, I finally realized that I can't force them to eat, so I stopped trying.

The testing and refusal to eat can start any time, and the struggle becomes more difficult as they get older. Many feeding struggles and difficulties can be avoided, like the ones that develop when a kid says, "I don't like that. Can I have a grilled cheese?" ... *and you make him a grilled cheese.* For me, this was a ridiculous request! It's hard enough to make one dinner for seven people. Can you imagine making more than one meal for dinner? I guess I was a little selfish because there was no way I was spending another twenty minutes of my precious and priceless time making an extra dinner that the kids would eat! If they didn't like something, they were more than welcome to eat it anyway, or wait until the next meal. This was a battle I was not going to fight. They had way more control of what and how much they ate, so I stayed out of it. I let them know that we would be eating another meal in four to eight hours and they could eat then. I guess it didn't hurt that I *really* disliked cooking, so the thought of more time in the kitchen made it *very* easy to say no to these requests.

If they are hungry, they will eat! It won't kill them to skip a meal or two. Even if they are on the smaller side, or don't gain weight easily. Unless there is a physical problem preventing them from eating enough or getting the necessary nutrients, it really isn't worth the battle of trying to make them eat. It's a waste of everyone's time to sit and wait for them, and a waste of energy playing the "you're not getting up until you finish your plate" game. It's much easier for you to let them make the choice. If they choose not to eat what has been prepared they will be hungry. Most likely they will remember this and will choose differently the next time. Even young kids, toddlers, and older babies can understand this concept. If it's an appetite issue, as it often is, you are powerless in trying to change it. If they just don't like the food, the decision is still theirs, although a more difficult decision for sure! It's especially difficult if dessert is presented as an option afterwards.

△ **TIP:** *Introduce the vegetables first, because they don't taste quite as good as the fruits. Also, when making baby food don't forget you can add vegetables like spinach and kale to fruit combinations.*

△ *When your older child says, "I don't like that! Can you make me something else?" Don't do it! It won't kill them to skip a meal, but it will likely be the beginning of something awful for you if you say yes.*

Dessert is an option that works well in our house, even to this day. I have to confess that we are very much a dessert-eating family. In our house, we serve "dessert" every night. One reason is to bribe the kids with dessert at dinner. Over the last several years, our kids have chosen to miss dessert on rare occasions because they didn't want to eat their dinner. It has been a very powerful bargaining tool. It also shifts control to them, which can be a powerful learning opportunity. Now, when I say dessert, I don't mean a milkshake, cookies, a bowl of ice cream every night. One night dessert would be a milkshake, and then ten M&Ms the next. Or maybe it was two big marshmallows for Reese, ten M&Ms for Jack, and a glass of chocolate milk for Ryanne. Sometimes dessert was, and continues to be a fruit smoothie with spinach, *but* topped with whipped cream. It really should be called a treat. It can be whatever you make it and it can be used in whatever way you feel is necessary, but it was often the great influencer at dinnertime.

"Feeding issues are most often behavioral in nature. Even if texture sensitivity exists, children learn to avoid certain textures, which exacerbates the problem, since it hinders skill development. Parents don't often know how much to push the issue, since refusal behaviors can become really intense."

— Michelle Sutherland, BCBA
(Board Certified Behavior Analyst)

Maybe they really don't like the food. Or maybe they are just *really* stubborn. It might even be that the texture of the food is undesirable. No matter the reason, forcing them to eat is not the answer. Mealtime should be relaxing and enjoyable. If you force them, they may learn to dislike eating. And the younger they are, the more vulnerable they are to developing this behavior issue. Allowing them a choice takes the focus off the parent and the meal, and puts more emphasis on the kids' decision.

Of our five children, only one has had feeding difficulties. Only one has had very *strong* opinions about food and textures. This is the result of several difficulties, most of which we had no control over. Had we kept putting the food and textures in front of him, even when he wasn't feeling his best, he might have been less aversive to food and textures. Had I known better, I would have introduced oral therapy much sooner, as most of Jesse's oral development was happening when he ate solids—and this didn't happen often. In hindsight, I realize how important it is to intervene as soon as possible, with any difficulty or delay. You will find a lot more detailed information on Jesse, his feeding difficulties, and his therapy in a later chapter.

△ *Allow them a choice during mealtime to take the focus off the parent and the meal, and to put more emphasis on the kids' decision.*

Feeding: Refusal and Behavior Issues

What if she is very young, doesn't want to eat, and starts throwing her food on the floor? The obvious response is usually to pick it up off the floor and offer it again. After all, she needs to eat and maybe she just dropped it, *right*? So, you put it on her tray and, oops, there it goes again, down to the floor. Well, this game has the potential to last for hours and generally doesn't end up with the kid eating. So you could play the game, *'cause that smile is just so darn cute*! Or, you could nip it in the bud right away, by taking her out of her chair and telling her "all done." This is a time when self-feeding is beginning, and she's learning to make choices and discover the consequences. Throwing food on the floor has never been allowed in our house, but it wasn't always easy taking them out of their seat and ending their meal. In fact, sometimes we didn't do it. We stayed as consistent as we could manage, and we managed to limit the food throwing to age two and younger.

Self Feeding at Twelve to Eighteen Months

Self-feeding is an exciting stage for everyone, but it's definitely messy. Whether your toddler is throwing his food on the floor, or just trying to get the yogurt in his mouth, the food generally doesn't end up where it should. If he demonstrates a desire to be more independent, let him! It can be tough because he will make huge messes and he will love it. Plus it's great for his hand/eye coordination. When Joe started working on his feeding skills, he was very insistent on doing it himself, and would not eat unless he got to use a spoon or a fork. He actually started eating a little better when he got to choose what and how much he ate. Even if he didn't eat everything, at least he always tried a bite.

Pay attention to when he is finished eating. Once he's full (or had enough), he may start to play. First the food will move from his plate or bowl to all over the tray, then the floor, then... the hair! There is nothing more frustrating than trying to get massive amounts of rice out of very fine, and extremely curly baby hair. If you're not a daily bath giver, as I am *not*, and/or you have lots of kids, a dinner mess to clean at bedtime, and a husband who works late, an extra unexpected bath is a total pain in the rear! Anything that sticks to the hands will be fun for babies to play with — yogurt, cream of wheat, oatmeal, you name it. So pay attention and avoid the extra clean up!

△ **TIP:** *Once they have finished their meal, or have had enough, remove their food from the tray or table. They may start to play. There is nothing more frustrating than removing massive amounts of rice or oatmeal from very fine, extremely curly baby hair.*

As the kids have gotten older they've learned to self-feed quite well. They know what to expect at dinner and at any meal, and they understand the consequence of skipping it. If they choose not to eat, it won't kill them. In our house, we let them choose. As they mature they get smarter and realize they don't like being hungry. They eat more dinners and skip fewer, and they feel like they are making their own decisions.

> "We did baby-led weaning and loved it! You definitely have to become comfortable with gagging and letting the baby figure out how to take bites and chew their food, but it's so nice when they get the hang of it."
>
> — Kacey, mother of 3

Dinnertime, and mealtime in general, is a struggle for many parents. Several of my friends talk about the frustration and drama that goes on during most of their family mealtimes. They complain about how much time they spend at the table trying to persuade their kid to eat, and then how they threatened them. Then when their kid doesn't eat, they wait, and wait and wait. It's difficult to listen to their complaints when I can't share their frustration. I try not to offer unsolicited ideas unless they want them. But waiting for my kids to eat their dinner is not even on my subconscious list of things to do. What mom has time for this?!

Be consistent, and don't reward them by giving in. It's not easy listening to them cry because they don't like the dinner and they're *so* hungry. When they ask you if you could *please* make them something else, it can be *very* difficult to say no, but, it doesn't take long for them to realize that they have to make the difficult choice to eat or not to eat. Dinner is made and waiting to be eaten and you are off the hook. Don't give in.

Feeding by breast, bottle, or spoon comes with its challenges. Over time these challenges become easier, and they are skills that can be mastered. When kids are little, it doesn't always seem like they will get there. With the right tools, realistic expectations, and information on what to expect, the feeding stages can be fun and exciting. Like any stage, they will come and go with little or no major challenges or surprises. When your kids do finally master the art of self-feeding, it will be yours and their great accomplishment. One that may allow you a few extra minutes a day to tackle something else. Independence is bliss, during childhood.

△ Notes

Five

Sleeping: From Bassinet To Big Kid Bed

Sleep habits, I believe, can be started as early as two **months.** It's all about preparing them slowly, and gently guiding them to become independent and comfortable being alone. It's one of the very important skills that will support the development of a healthy, confident adult. It's not always easy, and at times can be very frustrating, but it will be well worth the sweat and tears.

Some people refuse to let their babies cry themselves to sleep, yet are okay with the fact that their babies are unable to calm themselves or put themselves to sleep, which can severely limit a baby's ability to sleep through the night. It can be torturous to listen to your baby cry while helping him develop positive sleep habits. Is it better to avoid the agony of listening to your baby cry to prevent the struggle, or is it better for the baby or child to go through the difficult process of crying themselves to sleep, which often takes only a few weeks for them to adapt to a full night's sleep? This approach guides and teaches them to soothe themselves and to sleep when it's time to sleep. Some people use the term "cry it out," which I don't particularly like. It's more like guiding them to "work it out" themselves, while reassuring them that they are safe. I used this with all my children, and it has worked very well. My children are extremely happy, loved and adventurous, and

△ **FYI:** *I would rather go through a few weeks of torture, listening to my baby cry himself to sleep, than to spend a year or longer of not sleeping through the night myself because my baby wakes up all night long.*

they've been sleeping through the night since they were four months old. All of them! I realize many may disagree with my approach, and that's ok.

Sleep Training: Two to Three Months

I once read that it is rare if babies sleep through the night before they are a year old, and to expect it to take longer than a year. Where I read it, I can't recall, but it's very possible that it came from a mother who strongly objected to using the cry it out method. Who named this particular strategy for building independence, anyway? I don't understand why it's called cry-it-out. It sounds like a punishment and so much worse than what it really is, which is building independence and self-confidence. It really does work, and it has been one of my proudest achievements in parenting.

> **"Sleep training helped us to look forward to bedtime (kids and parents both!)"**
>
> **— Michelle S., mother of 3**

Every parent has his or her way of doing things, and it's usually never right or wrong. I must say, however, that I would rather go through a few weeks of torture, listening to my baby cry himself to sleep, than to spend a year or longer of not sleeping through the night myself because my baby wakes up all night long. Can you imagine going to work on less than five hours of sleep a night, for an entire year!? It's easier for stay-at-home moms to have less sleep because they don't have to get up and go to work. I'm sure many moms with newborns also have school aged children that require an early alarm. Do stay-at-home moms deserve any less sleep than working moms? All moms, and dads, deserve as much sleep as they can get. What would it feel like, as a parent, *to look forward to* bedtime and naptime, as opposed to dreading it like so many do? Well, it's *amazing!*

Looking back, I wouldn't do anything differently. We have five kids that sleep well, on their own, when it's time, and still have naps or "rest time" when we tell them to, or for the older ones when they need it. When I wrote this part our oldest was ten! Even now at thirteen, she understands the importance of sleep. I feel amazingly blessed and lucky that our kids have such great sleep skills. Not only is it great for me and my husband, as I'm sure you can imagine how hard it might be to have "us" time, but it's extremely healthy for our kids and their physical and emotional development. It has also made it much easier for others (grandparents, aunts, uncles) to say yes to watching our kids overnight.

> **"We did sleep training with our first son. It was the best thing we ever did!"**
>
> — **Danielle R., mother of 3**

Family hotel stays are much more pleasant when your kids can and do go to sleep when it's time. We've had a lot of weekends away from home for our daughters' soccer tournaments and other sporting events, so of course we stay in hotels. It's generally all seven of us in one small room with two beds and some floor space. Yes, I know—we are breaking the rules with too many people in one room. But do hotels really expect parents to pay double, for two separate rooms? It's definitely not vacation when we do this, but we manage. We do what is necessary to make the most of our family time, which is precious and nearly nonexistent. Now that the pack 'n play stage is over, we have more room to make beds on the floor. But no matter where they make their beds, the kids settle down when we tell them, and most of the time they go to sleep. We stay up watching TV and visiting, It's really nice that my hubby and I get to stay up late when we go on a trip and don't have to go to bed when our kids do.

> **"Sleep training...Bahahah, our kid still sleeps with us!"**
>
> — **Loni, veteran mother of 4**

Skills for sleeping, and I really believe this, begin to develop with the early introduction to the bassinet, and the transition from bassinet to crib. If you make this a slow process and try to prepare your baby for nighttime isolation, the crying will be short-lived, and you will have a baby that goes to sleep easily, sleeps well, and when older goes to bed when told, with very little struggle. Sound nice? It's more than nice, it's *amazing*! Naptime also becomes something to look forward to, and not a dreaded chore. It has been wonderful for my husband and I. The benefits to teaching your child good sleep habits are something to preach, and I'm doing just that!

Some positive results we've seen with our children are:

△ A healthier child.

△ Better attention during the day.

△ Better moods (and, boy, can we tell when they need more sleep!)

△ Easier nap and bedtime routines.

△ More time for you and your husband.

△ An early understanding of how important sleep is for everyone (kids and adults), which will help them make better choices later in life.

△ The comfort of being alone in the dark.

△ The ability for us as parents to really know when something isn't right (because they don't sleep well when they are sick, for instance).

I realize it's very difficult for some new moms and dads to put their new babies down. They want to hold them constantly, look at them, feed them all the time, sleep with them, play dress-up—well, just kidding on the last one, but creating a physical attachment so strong early on can make it very difficult for a baby to adjust when she isn't being held. This practice can make it tough when trying to get your baby to sleep alone. The desire for mothers to embrace their babies makes complete sense. It is a natural instinct that many mothers don't want to let go of their newborns. Newborns need the closeness as much as the mothers do. It is, however, important always to remember that some things, although difficult for both parent and child, are healthy and okay for baby.

Floor Time For Positive Sleep Habits

My babies spent a lot of their time on the floor, in the bassinet, and in a swing, but mostly on the floor. After just a few weeks I was putting them on the floor to let them stretch and move, and to give myself time to finish a chore. I wasn't able to use the floor as often with the last few because the older kids were usually rambunctious and dangerous. The couch was another fairly safe place for them to lie. It might be a good idea to desist from couch laying when they hit the roll-over stage. When little baby Joe was a little over four months old he decided to try rolling over. He was on the far inside edge of the couch on his back. After a few minutes of obvious distress, I looked over and saw him on his tummy doing the superman fly. He had one arm hanging over the edge of the couch and his legs were kicking. He had rolled from back to front and was an inch from rolling completely off the couch. Phew! He didn't fall but thankfully he'd graduated to the floor without a major crash.

After about six weeks, I started giving my kids a lot of floor time. A lot of holding and cuddling is no doubt one of the best things about parenting, and I did a lot of this too. It can create resistance to being alone. Easing them in slowly (as opposed to cold turkey) "floor time" can make it much easier for them to adjust. With out time or freedom to move, stretch or observe independently, they may have a more difficult time adjusting to new sleeping and even social situations. Constant holding can also delay a baby's physical development. For example, he may sit up very late, or struggle to roll over. His muscles won't develop as quickly or efficiently if he isn't given the time, and space to explore the floor.

Crib and Sleep

Our philosophy has always been that a crib means sleep, and we tried to teach this to our babies. A crib or bed in our house has never meant "time to eat." And it most definitely was never related to discipline.

As soon as our babies slept at least six hours, the two am, four am, or whatever time feeding was eliminated. Instead of giving them a bottle or breast when they woke up, I'd give them a binkie or rock them back to sleep. This was tough for a week or two. Some babies don't take pacifiers like other babies, and may need to be held until they fall back to sleep. It's extremely difficult to do this in the middle of the night when you are tired. It was much more than what we were prepared for, but we did it. To be completely honest, I did it. Sometimes we took turns getting up and staying up, but it really is the mom that tackles the midnight waking and rocking. This practice, I believe, was instrumental in developing our kids' good sleep habits early.

However, this type of training can and should be adjusted if your baby is having feeding difficulties, or struggling to gain weight. As I've said before, Jesse struggled to gain weight because he had feeding issues, which made eating more difficult for him. For this reason, he got to eat when he wanted, and

△ **TIP:** *Once they've slept all night, eliminate the nighttime feeding—unless they're sick or struggling to gain weight. If you feed them once at four am, you'll be feeding them every morning at four am until you break the habit. And once established, this can be very hard.*

Our bedtime philosophy for developing good sleep habits focused on these ideas:

△   No bottles in bed.

△   When "training" them to fall asleep in bed, don't take them out of bed until they have fallen asleep and have woken up (unless they are sick) even if it is a very short nap. If the result is a very short nap, but they have been asleep, it's okay to pick up.

△   Put in bed when sleepy but not when sleeping. This will teach them to fall asleep on their own so you aren't rocking them to sleep, or driving them in a car for hours on end.

△   Never use a bed or crib for punishment or play (that's what playpens are for). I did not want my kids to have a negative feeling about their resting place. I wanted them to want to go to bed.

△   If they wake at night let them cry a little before rushing in, but don't allow them to become hysterical. Try to avoid picking them up.

△   Once they've slept all night, eliminate the nighttime feeding—unless they're sick or struggling to gain weight. If you feed them once at four am, you'll be feeding them every morning at four am until you break the habit.

△   Use a binkie or pacifier...studies have shown that a binkie may reduce the risk of SIDS. The reliance on a binkie depends on how often the parent allows the child to have it. After four months, the binkie was only allowed at sleeping times and sickness.

for as long as he wanted. Unfortunately in his case, he slept all night and was never thrilled about waking up to eat.

Co-Sleeping

The term co-sleeping may be unfamiliar to new parents and there is no specific definition for the word. For this section, and in my experience as a mother of babies, the term co-sleeping refers to a baby sleeping in the same bed with mom, dad, or both parents. Some new parents prefer this for nerves and safety, mothers may find it better for breastfeeding and sleep, and some just want to be close to their little ones.

We avoided co-sleeping at all cost. This might be difficult for some new parents, but you really won't regret it. We had a lot of motivation to help us. We got some great advice from my mother. She once told me, when my sister was ten and still sleeping with her, "Don't *ever* bring them into your bed or you'll get a Julia!" This was enough to convince me! After all, my sister Julia was baby number six, and my mom *knew* she had created a monster. Suffice it to say, we *never* had our kids sleeping with us. Other reasons to keep baby out of your bed are:

△ Better sleep for you and baby.

△ When it does happen, because of illness or a nightmare, it's much more special for everyone.

△ A healthier relationship with your partner.

△ Successful sleepovers or overnight babysitting because they are comfortable sleeping alone.

△ Safer for baby (there are risks with co-sleeping).

It was very important to us that our kids felt calm, safe, and peaceful when it was time to go to bed. We avoided giving bottles in bed because we did not want to confuse them. Bedtime and mealtime should be completely separate. Otherwise they may associate their bed with eating, more than sleeping. If a baby's punishment involves crib time, he will start associating his bed with negative feelings and guilt, and he'll hate it. His bed should be a place of peace, comfort, calmness, and rest. Yes, there were lots of times—many times, they were angry

△ *There were a lot of times our kids were angry or upset about going to bed, but there is a big difference between protesting bedtime and fearing it.*

and upset about going to bed, but there is a big difference between protesting bedtime and fearing it.

Another important guideline we set was that our babies understood the importance of bedtime, and that staying in bed was expected. Babies and toddlers need to know their boundaries, and it should be very clear what the goal is. Although babies don't understand goals, older kids do, and as they get older they start to connect the dots. Our rule was, once in bed, they stayed. We wanted to create boundaries and limits so they got the necessary ten to twelve hours of sleep. We also tried to avoid spending hours getting them to stay. Without boundaries, bedtime can be a nightmare and last for hours, when the routine itself needs only thirty minutes or less. This includes getting dressed, brushing teeth, water, story time, and a goodnight kiss. Boundaries that are established early, and get plenty of consistent practice, will positively influence the routine. When the age of climbing and testing comes, they will be much more likely to stay in bed and will get the sleep they need. When they decide to test and get out without permission, it is much easier to remind them what the rule is and why staying in bed is so important. A bonus is that you and your spouse or partner will get the sleep, affection, conversation, or whatever it is that *you* need.

Our two oldest, both girls, never tried to climb out of their crib and stayed in their big beds without much involvement from us. At five and six years old, they still stayed in bed until they had our permission to get up, whether they needed the bathroom or a drink of water. As they got older, they tested a little, always needing one more drink or one more kiss, but they were beginning to understand the importance of getting enough sleep, and they started making better choices on their own. Jack was a different story, and we did get involved a little when he started climbing out of his crib. The same happened and was bound to happen with his brothers.

Our babies were sleeping through the night when they were four months old, with the exception of Jesse. Jesse needed special treatment because of his weight issues, and other health troubles. Although he wasn't sleeping all night long, he did fall asleep on his own from a very early age. I believe personality has a lot to do with a child's tendency, fears, and struggles, but I believe a challenging child, especially when it comes to bedtime, can be "trained" to sleep well and independently.

This skill for the more difficult child will give him a tremendous amount of self-confidence. It tells a kid a lot about himself when he can feel okay when he's alone, and in the dark, and the added confidence is all the more reason to succeed in helping him build this skill.

We started encouraging healthy sleep habits before they transferred from bassinet to crib, and we did this by introducing them to the bassinet early. We provided them with lots of opportunities to spend time awake in the bassinet, so that when the transition period was nearing, naptime would be easier. After several weeks of napping and sleeping comfortably in the bassinet, moving to a crib was the obvious and fairly easy next step. Once they graduated to a crib, we made it very clear that once in bed, they would not be coming out until they fell asleep (or had a very nice, long, peaceful rest). This was not easy—especially when they didn't want to nap and they cried for hours. I say they because they *all* did it!

When Ryanne permanently transitioned to her crib for naptime, she was three months old. She was our first baby, and we did a mediocre job in preparing her for the transition. We put her in her crib cold turkey, with no warming up to it and no opportunities for play. She hadn't even spent five minutes in her crib before we threw her in there for her first nap in her new bed. We were relentless, and she cried for three hours straight! Of course we ran in to check on her every five minutes initially, and then spaced our visits a little more each time, but we never took her out. I had to physically restrain Daddy several times so he wouldn't run in and ruin her training. We never gave in and did our best to comfort her and to make her feel safe. For several days we worked on her training. With each day, her protests became shorter, until she finally realized she wasn't coming out until she rested. We too, were better able to resist the urge to take her out. After a few weeks of torture—for us—the crying stopped. After this, naptime was a breeze and bedtime too.

I'm not going to tell you that she never tested us again. Boy, did she! Every few months she would try her luck at protesting. She'd cry a little, then a lot, but it never lasted longer than ten minutes, and she only tried for a few days. And again, she'd realize she was stuck! I talk a lot about stages in this book, and I feel each stage is their exploration and attempt to push the boundaries. As parents we must try to stay consistent in our expectations. If we do, the stages will be just that, a stage, and they will eventually pass. Up until our oldest was eight, she wouldn't get out of bed without asking us first. If she wanted to change her pajamas, she asked. If her baby doll fell on the floor, and she wanted to get it, she'd ask. We've always wondered how long it would last and when our kids would realize that they could get out of bed any time they wanted. Maybe they already knew this and just chose to stay in bed because they knew it was best. The latter is how I see it. At ten, Ryanne started to get out of bed without asking, but it was usually with good reason. She was old enough to make those choices. I guess that's why most nights she chose to go to bed before we asked her. Reese was also very good at going to bed when she was ready. As teenagers, or almost, it's becoming a different story.

We had similar training situations with the other kids, but because we were more experienced parents, I think we made the transition a little easier by introducing the crib a little at a time. Bedtime with our other children was equally as easy and gratifying. The training was slightly different, because we knew better how to handle the feelings of doubt and failure. We experienced the same worries, the same heartache and the same amount of tears, but we also enjoyed the same gratification of success! When each child stopped crying that first, horrible day, we felt victorious and proud that we made it through. Each day after, as they cried less and less, we felt increasingly excited that it was almost over. After this difficult period, the bedtime routine was easy, calm, and usually pretty peaceful. As a mom, I'm very proud of this accomplishment, and feel even more satisfied that my children get the sleep they need every night—especially after starting grade school, as sleep became noticeably more important.

Sleeping Habits at Age Two to Three Years: From Crib to Big Kid Bed

What happens when they graduate from a crib to a big kid bed? Well, with each new transition, we feared the worst. What kid would stay in bed if they could get out easily? I'll never know how we got so lucky, but our two oldest never tried to get up from their big kid beds. Like I said, even at eight and six, they always asked before they got out of bed, and we very rarely saw them in the middle of the night. They did try their luck at sleeping with mom and dad, but we simply picked them up and took them back to their own beds. On special occasions, or during illnesses, earaches, coughs, or the occasional nightmare, we of course, let them sleep with us. What kind of heartless parents do you think we are!? It only happened once in a while. We tried to avoid creating a habit. Let me tell you, creating a habit happens much easier and quicker than breaking one!

Maybe it wasn't luck, but more a result of the boundaries and expectations we set when they were babies. Whatever the reason, they stayed in bed and bedtime was easy. I know many moms that dread bedtime and constantly struggle with kids getting out of bed. Before Jack, I really couldn't say how I would feel if we had to deal with this nightly routine.

When Jack turned two we had our first glitch in the bedtime routine. Our wacky, curious little boy realized he didn't have to wait for someone to get him and he started to climb out of his crib on his own! His departure from his crib occurred both at night, and during naptime. As I heard his little foot-steps on the tile floor, around 2:00 am, I expected to hear his sister say, "I'm scared," but what I heard was a very quiet voice that said, "mamma?" Of course we were shocked and soon after we were brainstorming and arguing about what we were going to do. Long story short, it took about five days, but when Jack tiptoed in we walked him back. And again, he tiptoed in and we walked him back. He wasn't happy, and he protested dramatically, with kicks and screams, and the "I'm scared" plea. After a week or so he was no longer climbing out of his crib. Once again, we put him in bed and he stayed. Two weeks later, he graduated to a big boy bed. Of course, we expected him to get out of bed and come find us, but this

△ *When Jack turned two, our wacky, curious little boy realized he didn't have to wait for someone to get him and he started to climb out of his crib on his own!*

didn't happen. He stayed in bed and consistently went to bed easily, until he turned three. When he turned three, curiosity overcame him and he tried it again, and Daddy waivered.

Jack started coming into our room every morning around three. Daddy would grab him and bring him into bed. I usually protested, because I couldn't sleep with Jack's feet digging into my back. I also didn't want him to do it every morning because it was going to affect his sleep. Unfortunately, my protests were ignored and I quit fighting—I was tired! An argument wasn't all that appealing at three in the morning either. It became a daily event, occurring usually between three and four every morning. It went on for a few months until we realized how bad it was for Jack to wake up so early. I also reminded my husband that early morning sex was out of the question, as long as Jack was in our bed!

> "With both kids, we transitioned them from crib to bed when we were nervous they could or would climb out of their crib. Their first big kid bed was a mattress on the floor with a foam pool noodle under the fitted sheet, to help prevent them from rolling off."
>
> — Theresa, mother of 2

The unfortunate thing about this situation is that we had to retrain him. He was doing so well, and we let the bad habit stay long enough for Jack to get accustomed to it. It was a lot harder to kick the habit than it would have been to nip it right away! I, however, had no part in the retraining. The funny thing about kids is that they are smart. Jack knew that if he came into our room and to my side of the bed, I would take him back to bed. So he started going to Daddy's side of the bed because he knew Daddy would say yes. Lucky for me, when Daddy started taking him back to bed, I was off the hook, and never had to do a thing. I made it clear to my husband that it was not my doing and that I would not be losing any sleep over the situation. It took close to two weeks to get Jack back to staying in bed. Every morning, at least twice,

Daddy would take him back to his room, with some kicking and screaming from Jack and very little conversation, but with a lot of love and empathy. It was like a groundhog morning where the same scenario repeats itself over and over each new day. For us it was two times a morning, every morning, for two weeks in a row. I wasn't tired, but my husband almost didn't make it. Eventually it became significantly less. After two or three months, Jack tried it only once a week, and then stopped coming in altogether.

Jesse's graduation to a big kid bed happened before I was really ready. I never thought I'd be celebrating the day one of my kids climbed out of his crib. This day was long awaited and extremely exciting for us. Of course, we knew Jesse needed a bed, but we dreaded the all too familiar transition from baby to big boy. We had been there before with three, and the most recent, Jack, was very tough. We thought it might be easier with Jesse because he didn't seem as strong-willed—or at least he didn't vocalize it because of his speech delays. We also thought it might be more difficult because it was possible that Jesse would not understand what he was expected to do. But, a week after climbing out of his crib, Jesse had his new Thomas the Train toddler bed. He loved it! His first three nights went great! We put him to bed, and he stayed and drifted off to sleep peacefully. Now, these three nights were weekdays, and Jesse was always really tired after his long, action packed days at preschool (where he often missed or misused his naptimes). His exhausted little body couldn't physically protest the bedtime. The fourth day was a Saturday, so we were home. Home for his first nap in his new bed ...

A Naptime Protest

I put him down at one, then he got up. I put him back. He got up. I put him back. For about two hours, Jesse toyed with my emotions and had a great time doing it. I stayed calm, which has always been the key to winning! And Jesse got flustered and upset, which is usually a good sign that they are weakening. About an hour after he started showing his emotions, he gave up and fell asleep—in his bed! I won, I won! Oh, and it was a sweet victory.

One Saturday my husband and I did a tag-team battle. We started at 1:30 and ended at 4:30. This three-hour battle included over 100 trips to the bed (just guessing—I didn't count), several minutes of teeth grinding, and a good hour of husband and wife bickering over whose turn it was and who had spent more time putting him back in bed. Jesse smiled, laughed, and jumped around for most of the three hours. Not strong-willed? This kid had more willpower and determination than I'd ever seen! It was frustrating, tiring, and to be honest, a little exciting. It was also scary. If we didn't win, we'd be doing this at every naptime, and if we couldn't do it with Jesse, how would we do it with Joe. Like the last time, with about an hour left of strength, Jesse started to show signs of weakness. He cried a little, tried to hit a few times, and cried some more. Finally, exhaustion defeated him! Or we did. Either way, it was a win-win. I wish I could say that naptimes got easier for Jesse, and that he realized he had to stay put, but they did not, and he did not.

What I *have* noticed is that when Jesse is tired, he never gets out and he quickly goes to sleep. When he is not tired, or is just a little tired, he gets up over and over again. Sometimes he never goes to sleep. I've realized that, like my older kids, if Jesse just rests or has quiet time in his room, he will understand what is expected, and will continue to comply with nap and rest time. If the child doesn't necessarily need a rest time, I can almost guarantee the parents do!

Please remember that every kid will try to challenge you at least once after they've been trained for sleeping. A trained baby that has been going to bed quietly, without a fuss since three months old can and will test you. In my experience, it typically happens around six months, later at nine to twelve months, and sporadically as they get older. With Joe he tried it again at around fourteen months. It's possible it could be teething, or an illness, but generally if it's screaming at the beginning of a nap or at bedtime, he's likely just trying it out. He's probably thinking, "How long will it take for them to get me?" It feels a lot like the first few days of sleep training, and it can last a few days to a week or two. It's very confusing because at first it seems like something is wrong. So you go in and check, and he's fine, so you leave. And he screams and screams. Just know that it is likely just a test. Stay strong and don't give in. It too shall pass.

If your baby or child has been sleeping really well and then starts waking up a lot at night, it could be an illness or discomfort from teething. As I said earlier, a child who sleeps well but suddenly starts waking several times a night, is much easier to understand than a child who has never slept well. What I mean is that it is much easier to identify if there is an issue or discomfort because you can recognize the disturbance of sleep as out of the ordinary. A child that never sleeps well is much more difficult to read because the constant waking is typical, and the issue or illness may go unnoticed. How my kids sleep has always given me so much information about how they are feeling. It takes about two to three days for me to "diagnose" the problem. When they are young and aren't sleeping well, it's typically been teething, an ear infection, an upset stomach, or an illness. It was this way with all five of my kids, so I really feel it's important to share my perspective on this point.

Nothing is ever easy with children, and getting them to bed is no exception. Starting early is the key. They will have lots of practice when they are young, and bedtime will be a piece of cake by the time they hit preschool and beyond, and they will be getting a healthy amount of sleep. Equally important is that you, the parents, will get a healthy amount of whatever it is that you need.

△ *FYI: A child that sleeps well but suddenly starts waking several times a night is much easier to understand than a child that has never slept well.*

△ Notes

_____

_____

_____

_____

_____

_____

_____

_____

Six

Discipline

Disciplining our kids has been one of the toughest pieces of parenting. It doesn't get much easier as they get older—actually it gets more difficult. It's easy to *plan* how we will react but every child is different—in personality and willingness to test the boundaries. I have seen almost everything and at times, I still feel unsure when the time comes to lay down the law. Even the most logical solution may not come to mind until the moment has passed.

For example, what should a parent do if little Jack is standing in the tub, scooping up water, and dumping it straight onto the floor? While, I should add, Big Sister is in the tub with him and doesn't say a word until the bathroom floor has passed the flood stage? Well, I'll tell you what *I* did. I grabbed the little guy, dried him off, and sent him to bed. I also sent his sister to bed without dessert. Now right or wrong, who knows— but does it really matter? I wasn't terribly confident with the decision because I don't like creating a negative association with their beds and bedtime, but in the heat of the moment, that's all that came to my mind. I wasn't mean, or physical, and I explained to them why they were going to bed without dessert or a book, and I stuck to it! Then I wondered, as I did often with discipline, *Do they understand? Did they know it was wrong? Was I wrong?* If you haven't noticed or already figured it out, second-guessing is a trademark parenting practice. We all do it, and we all continue on regardless.

Time-out

Timeout is a traditional method of discipline used by many parents. Some call it the "think tank" or "quiet time." Whatever the name, it can be very effective if used appropriately. What happens when the good old "time-out" backfires, and you find yourself becoming increasingly frustrated and angry, because your two-year-old has finally realized he can get up? It's not easy putting a two-year-old in time-out. Most kids don't just give in and say, "ok mom, I'll just sit right here, without moving until you come get me out." If only it were that easy. It was that easy with our first two children, who never fought a time-out or even questioned it. But when Jack was two, after he'd finally learned to stay put and that time-out was not a good place, he started to explore his options. Not only did he start getting up again, but he also added dancing and mocking to his routine. He would jump up, dance around, and say, "nah, nah, nah nah nah." When I wasn't laughing, or was trying really hard to hide it, I got near the point of crazy. The picking up and putting back routine became increasingly rough and more physical until I began to feel guilty.

> **"My first two kids were pretty easy to discipline. My third baby is the most adventurous, able, full of energy kid I have ever met. Often I would lose my patience and at times what he was doing was potentially dangerous to him. We've done a lot of 'time to think' with him but as he has matured he is understanding boundaries better."**
>
> **— Kacey, mother of 3**

After my first experience with his dancing and blatant disregard for his punishment, yes he was only two, I realized that getting frustrated was the worst thing for the situation. The next time I tried a new approach and it worked. I call it "ignoring him." It supports the "ignore the bad, praise the good" philosophy. So I ignored his irritating behavior but was aware of what he was doing. I paid attention when he got up to move, and reacted quickly to put him back, but I ignored any annoying or irritating behavior during this process. When he saw that I was holding it together, and with confidence, he started staying put. Hallelujah! It is, however, very important to remove them from time-out within a reasonable amount of time. What I learned from television, and one magazine article from *Parenting Magazine* is that time-out should only be as many minutes as they are in age.

Naps and Discipline

This same strategy of ignoring the bad works very well when trying to reinforce the naptime routine. Unfortunately, when kids reach a certain age, and it's different for all of them, they start to test boundaries and defy rules and routine. It's the terrible twos stage, which comes up in more detail in a later chapter. But, the age of three to three and a half can be outrageously difficult—much more difficult than the age of two.

When Jack was three, he decided he wasn't going to listen and was going to try a different approach. He chose to deliberately disobey. We felt it most at naptime. I'm still surprised by how sudden it was. My sweet little boy went from angel to demon overnight! This is no exaggeration. I think he woke up one morning and decided it was time for him to run the show. Nap time went from our rules to his. For a first timer, this can be SO tough, especially if mom is pregnant or caring for an infant. We were ready, yet I say this with uncertainty.

On day two of his new circus show, I started taking away an item from his room every time I had to take him back in. I carried him or dragged him back to his room, without speaking to him, and left with a pillow. Five pillows later, I left with his blankets. Three blankets and an empty bed later, I realized it wasn't working so I spanked him hard. I spanked him so hard, I left a handprint on his upper thigh. I left his room feeling terrible and defeated, and on the verge of tears. Needless to say, he never took a nap that day and I was stressed out and at a loss for what to do. I dreaded day three. By day five, I was at the end of my rope. I felt like a rookie parent with absolutely no idea how to handle my child. What could I threaten or take away if he didn't stay in bed? Again, naptime started off rough. I threatened no dessert and an early bedtime. But did a two

△ *My sweet little boy went from angel to demon overnight! This is no exaggeration. I think he woke up one morning and decided it was time for him to run the show. Naptime went from our rules to his.*

year old really understand that type of reasoning? Of course I didn't really know, and he wasn't responding the way I hoped he would. He kept getting out of bed and running for the back door. I ran after him and carried him back to his room. After a few times, frustrated, I gave him a rough slap on his bottom, and he stayed for a few minutes. After a temporary retreat, he started again.

If you haven't been through this before you can't imagine my frustration, however, I decided to adjust my tactics and began ignoring him but keeping him in his room. If he started out of his door, I walked toward it, but would not look at him. Sometimes he would turn and run back in and sometimes I walked him back. He didn't get upset until the tenth or eleventh time, and then he started to cry. *This was a good sign,* I thought, because he's starting to get it. So far, the process had taken thirty minutes, but I stayed calm, never said a word to him, and avoided eye contact. If I did look at him, it was only to give him a very stern stare, but it was quick.

△ *He didn't get upset until the tenth or eleventh time, and then he started to cry. This was a good sign, I thought, because he's starting to get it. Don't give up!*

Eventually, I didn't have to take him back in because if he got out of his bed and headed to the door, I walked toward his room and he'd run to his bed and jump. Each time he did this, he threw his head into the pillow and cried some more. It became very easy to stay calm and simply walk toward him—*I was winning*. He was weakening and I was winning! It wasn't difficult to ignore him and after forty-five minutes, crying on the floor of his room, he rolled over and fell asleep. It was a huge VICTORY for me. I was relentless and determined to win that battle, and it paid off! After that day, Jack went back to his usual naptime routine. As parents, we must celebrate *every* success.

Siblings

I'm not sure this fits in the chapter, but like the topic itself, I don't have an answer. Sibling rivalry can create a mountain of discipline issues. Sadly, for most of these issues I have very little advice to give. But at the least, I hope my stories inspire a laugh, or a reminder that you are not alone.

Try to imagine, if you dare, a houseful of kids—five to be exact — all under the age of thirteen. Granted, we planned it this way, but *oh my gosh*! What were we thinking?! Obviously we didn't examine and plan for personalities, sibling chemistry, and gender conflicts. What parent would? But I had no idea it would be this tough! It's really only the oldest three that drive me near insanity. I would not change the dynamic for anything in this world, but I may not make it through the next round of boys.

The one question I am always asking myself is, "*What do I do?*" What do I do when they tattle because someone is blowing in their ear, or when the oldest of the boys is doing everything he can to push his sister's buttons, and she won't stop screaming at him. Seriously, what do I do? On one hand, I want to teach Reese patience, and the ability to ignore. On the other hand, little brother needs to be put in his place so he doesn't get punched later. So far, I've given Reese permission to hit her brother if he won't stop bugging her. I have also told her to warn him first, so he has a chance to stop. Is it surprising that she takes every opportunity to hit him? Then it becomes a full on brawl that, if you think about it, I started.

> "Consistency, picking my battles, and making sure that the consequences are appropriate and relevant to the problem behavior that occurred. These are my focus when dealing with behavior issues."
>
> — Michelle S., mother of 3

What kind of mother tells her kids to hit each other? Here again is the question, *What do I do*? Although the fighting is only really bad when we are all home together, ha. Which happens to be my vacation time. Being a teacher, I have a lot of vacation time, or better said, more time at home. I am very lucky to have the time I do with my family. I am also thankful I have a job outside the home to keep me connected to the world. But when my vacation from one job translates into overtime for the other, life can get a bit overwhelming.

On the flip side, we are blessed with moments of kindness and cooperation. It melts my heart to remember when they used to play house and called each other honey and mama. And they did this for many years when they were young. It's these moments that help me forget all the fighting, and bring me back to why we wanted a big family. Sadly, when these moments happen, they are short-lived.

Our family has two girls and three boys. The two girls are the oldest, and naturally, they fight horribly! Over EVERYTHING! They tattle, hit, borrow without asking, push each other's buttons, secretly wish the other would get sick, and who knows what else. Whether it's fighting over a specific color of cup (they really only did this when they were younger), or annoying one another by touching, copying, or singing loudly, it always ends in a screaming match; which usually turns into tattling. Now imagine trying to manage an argument or fight every five minutes. It's exhausting! And it brings me to re-examine my parenting daily, because I never really know if what I'm doing is right. A lot of it isn't, I'm sure. But one thing I do feel confident about is putting the pressure on them to make smart choices.

△ *Kids need to understand that they can't control others, or situations, or what happens in life. But they can control how they act, and how they react to what happens.*

> **"Taste your words before you eat them. In other words, think before you speak."**
>
> — Katie, mother of 1

I talk a lot about choices, giving choices, and explaining the consequences of a bad choice. For this I give credit to the strategies of Love and Logic. Love and Logic is a parenting program written and presented by Jim Fay. As the title suggests, it provides parenting tools that focus on using love and logic to teach kids responsibility. It is worth purchasing. I try to remind them to worry about their actions and not the actions of others. They need to understand that they can't control others, or situations, or what happens in life. But they can control how they act, and how they react to it all. Yes, they are very young, and don't understand much about life. But they do understand actions and consequence. Just the other day I heard Jack say to his cousin "That wasn't a very good choice."

The same thing is true about us as parents. We can't control our kids at any age. As they get older they start to realize this very powerful phenomena, and they start to test it. We hope as parents, that if we always put the power in their hands, or at least if they think it is, they may be more willing to trust us and what we teach them. Hopefully, when they are confronted with one of life's temptations, they will trust their hearts to make the right choice. I've seen it work very well, and I truly believe it is the reason we haven't had many discipline issues as they've gotten older. However, I can't stress enough the importance of consistency and perseverance when parenting, and especially in discipline. These will always be the best mediator, if used fairly.

> "Connection is key. With discipline a child will not become bitter toward the parent if there is love."
>
> — Katrina, veteran mother of 4

Consequences must be a part of disciplinary action with kids, and they are an integral part of teaching the appropriate behavior and helping right a wrong. There are many different types of consequences that many parents use. Some work very well and others often spark further rebellion. As I shared earlier, time-out is a consequence that can be very effective, if used appropriately. However, this only works for younger kids who are still dependent and without a lot of privileged activities. On the other hand, the *Go to your room!* response, which we have used often, does not always serve its intended purpose. Kids play, watch television or device videos, (if they have access), or they become distracted, preventing them from connecting their action with the consequence. When our kids were very young, we used time-out, loss of dessert and early bedtime, to name a few that worked. Now, and as they get older, the stakes are higher. Losing a cell phone or device for a period of time is an earth shattering consequence for a teenager. Equally devastating is missing a sports activity or canceling a play date with a friend. Anything that is fun, or something they look forward to is grounds for removal. We

△ **FYI:** *Anything that is fun, or something they look forward to is grounds for removal. However, consequences must also be actions you are wiling to take or privileges you are willing to remove.*

have found these to be very effective. However, consequences must also be actions you are willing to take, or privileges you are willing to remove.

Here is the reality, and what we have learned on the job. In the heat of the moment, shouting out a loss of privilege is easy. Actually following through with the threat is hard. To be honest, it can feel like a life or death decision. For example, when Ryanne and Reese were ten and nine, they got into a fight that led to screaming, kicking, and throwing things. We threatened that if they did not stop screaming, they would go to their rooms and we would not be going to the zoo the following day.

The first mistake we made, was thinking we could control their fighting by *making* them stop. We did not think about offering them options, or helping them to come up with a compromise to teach this important life lesson. The other mistake was that we threatened to ruin our family day at the zoo, when we weren't willing to follow through with it. This was a big consequence that would have affected everyone. A better, more appropriate option, would have been to threaten their TV time, which would have only affected them, and would have been a very easy privilege to take away, making it easy to follow through. We have since learned this, yet still find ourselves in chartered but uncertain territory. What has helped us and continues to keep us in the game, is discussing possible consequences for our kids before the event actually happens. We also give ourselves time to "think on it," which also gives the kids the same, and allows us to come up with an appropriate response.

△ *Give yourself time to "think on it," so your child can do the same. It will give you time to cool down and come up with an appropriate response.*

"Ask why the deed was done. The intent of the act is more important than the act itself. If we do not understand, good intentions may go punished and everyone loses."

— Rachel, *personal* childhood memory

I reiterate the importance of consistency and perseverance in enforcing discipline that works. You must be willing to give the punishment and see it through. It takes mental and emotional toughness, and you will want to give in, but don't do it! Like the other difficult moments in parenting, and like sleep training, it will be worth it. They will learn from their poor choices and you will feel good about being those parents that follow through. Patience in "sticking to your guns" will allow you to enjoy the victories when they do finally happen. As the kids get older, the victories will be so much more meaningful, and hopefully will require less of your involvement. By staying consistent and doing what you say, and allowing yourself to give up a little control, you will nourish your mental toughness and potentially reduce many of your family's discipline issues.

Before ending this chapter, I must also briefly revisit the idea of ignoring the bad and praising the good—the strategy that got me through so many tough toddler moments during bedtime, naptime, and many other tough times of parenting. I'm not suggesting that we ignore the bad choices and behavior. What we want from our children is for them to make good choices that lead to more good choices, positive thoughts, and consistently good behavior and positive actions. Wouldn't it make sense to reward and praise the positive things we see, emphasizing these types of decisions, instead of always giving a consequence? I have heard often in my parenting resources and teaching seminars that we must catch them doing something good, and celebrate it! So I say, let's do the celebrating instead. In our many years of parenting, we have found that praising the things they do that are good, for example completing a small chore or sharing with their siblings, motivates and inspires them to do more of these positive actions. It just makes sense, *doesn't it*?

△ **FYI:** *I have heard often in my parenting resources and teaching seminars that we must catch kids doing something good, and celebrate it! So I say, let's do the celebrating instead.*

△ Notes

Seven

Illness

A sick child, of any kind, is scary, exhausting, and many times tough to handle. If it's not a cold or cough, it's diarrhea or it's vomiting. Not in the toilet of course, but the vomit generally ends up all over themselves, their beds, car seats, carpet, and couch. Very rarely does a kid get sick in the bathroom, or, at least it doesn't happen when they are little. Kids aren't great at predicting when they might get sick, and there is really no way to know for sure if and when it will happen. When he seems sluggish and says his tummy hurts it would be wise to grab a bowl or bag, sometimes a towel, or two, and keep them close. If he does end up throwing up, sleeping on the bathroom floor next to him might allow you to sleep a little. If in bed or on the floor, a towel next to or underneath him is helpful, and you can expect to be up most of the night.

I was picking my kids up at my mom's, after work one afternoon. Reese came home early from school that day with a fever. Ryanne joined her because she "felt" sick. When I walked in and saw that the girls were at my moms', I realized I might be in for a difficult night. I had two with a fever, one with really bad diarrhea, one who said he didn't feel good, and one who was worrying that she was next. My husband was out of town.

We got home, walked in, and headed straight for the couch, first watching *Gnomio and Juliet*, and then *Full House*. Some ate dinner and some didn't. Jesse wanted to go to bed first. Then I put Joe to bed. Then Jack, with his tummy ache, said he was going to bed. The girls stayed up and did homework while I sat with them and did my own. Twenty minutes later we all hear what sounds like water being dumped on the floor. The noise came from Jack's room.

You can probably guess that it was not water. It was Jack throwing up over the side of his bed, half asleep, all over the carpet. He threw up three times, big ones, before I could even attempt to save the carpet from any more vomit. Later when I was cleaning sheets, floor, more floor, carpet, and more carpet, I pulled open his drawer (his bed had three pull out drawers underneath), and what did I find? A puddle of vomit on the bottom of his drawer. Yuck! I spent forty-five minutes scrubbing, wiping, spraying, and it still smelled like peanut butter and jelly, and vomit. With all the excitement of the night, I almost forgot about work the next day, and what I was going to do with my sick kids.

Fevers

△ *We learned the scary way, with Ryanne, that fevers are different for everyone. A fever of 102 for one child might be 105 for another, yet the severity is the same. It is the child's behavior along with the fever that will determine the severity.*

Fevers are important to understand because they are common, but they are scary. They fluctuate, and they can be very dangerous. If you expect them, and prepare, they are very manageable and much less worrisome. We learned the scary way, with Ryanne, that fevers are different for everyone. A fever of 102 for one child might be 105 for another, yet the severity is the same. When Ryanne was nine months old she had an allergic reaction to an antibiotic. She broke out in hives and started running a fever. Her fever came before the hives and it quickly got to 105. We were freaking out and of course we called the on-call doctor. The doctor asked us how she was acting. She was obviously not feeling well, but she wasn't acting delirious or out of it. The doctor told us to give her a dose of Tylenol. He said to alternate Tylenol with Motrin, and to put her in a lukewarm bath to help with the fever. He also told us that it's not how high the fever reads that is important, but how the child is acting. Severe lethargy can indicate a more serious problem, and he told us to watch her behavior.

When she started getting the hives about an hour later, we took her in to the emergency room. When we told the nurse that her fever had been 105, she scolded us for not bringing her in. A classic example of differing medical opinions, and a good reason for new parents like us to panic. So, we panicked a little, but learned our lesson. Don't always trust the first thing the doctor says. Doctors don't always agree, and they never understand your child like you do. After this first trip to the ER, we learned that when Ryanne got sick we could usually expect a very high fever. And that's generally what we got. Now with Reese and our other kids, their fevers never went above 102.

Several years later we found out that we had two kids with an allergy to penicillin. When Joe was thirteen months old, he saw a pediatrician—not his—who prescribed amoxicillin for an ear infection. This medication was a ten day three times a day antibiotic, which is tough to carry out in full. He started getting a very small rash, but nothing big. When we went back to the doctor to check Joe's ears we asked the doctor about it. He said a rash is typical with a viral infection like a cold. So we dismissed it. His ears were unchanged so the doctor prescribed Augmentin, which is a stronger anti-biotic with more penicillin. It too was a ten day antibiotic, but only twice a day. After six days of taking this, Joe woke up one morning, covered in small red bumps. As the day went on, the bumps started pooling together, becoming large, raised groups of bumps, and then hives. By 5:00 that night, he was covered head to toe in large red hives, and we were at the doctor for the third time in three weeks. We saw Joe's pediatrician who prescribed Benadryl, and a steroid to help with the swelling. She also prescribed the antibiotic we usually get for the kids—Azithromycin, which is a five day, once-a-day treatment. The next day Joe's hives were so much better, and we realized how important it is to keep Benadryl on hand, just in case. This experience also prompted us to find a back up pediatrician we trusted, so we would feel comfortable taking the kids to a different doctor. Finding a new doctor opened up more time slots and avail-ability when scheduling.

△ *A classic example of differing medical opinions, and a good reason for new parents like us to panic. So, we panicked a little, but learned our lesson. Don't always trust the first thing the doctor says. Doctors don't always agree, and they never understand your child like you do.*

The Common Cold

Next on the list of common child illnesses is the cold. A cold generally starts with a clear, runny nose. Then the clear stuff turns green and yucky! A cough is sometimes part of it, and it starts small and can get phlegmy. Lots of phlegm doesn't usually mean dangerous, as long as the coughing is doing its job. This means that the cough is productive and clearing the chest and lungs of the gunk. If the cough is weak, or if it becomes constant, and persistent, it should be checked. The cough can also sound loud and similar to a barking dog. This type of cough is very scary, but usually nothing to worry about. It's often called "croup" and can sometimes cause difficulty breathing. Try not to panic. This type of cough usually comes at night, so take them outside and let them breath the cold air. Also, use the steam from a hot shower. This may take a little longer than walking outside, but it too can really help clear the lungs for better breathing.

If the cough persists for several days to weeks and is accompanied by a slight fever, you will want to have the lungs examined by a doctor. Pneumonia is very difficult to identify, even for a trained physician. It is not always heard in the lungs or diagnosed without a chest x-ray. If the cough persists, a fever is present, and the baby or child is showing signs of lethargy, take him in.

"Croup was a tough 'first' for us. I remember I panicked with our first baby. When the other two kiddos got croup like symptoms we stayed calm, walked outside in the cold, and used essential oils."
— Kacey, mother of 3

Also with a cold, which is usually a viral infection and does not require antibiotics, comes a sore throat. These are hard to diagnose from a parents observation, but they can be very painful. During one of Jesse's recent colds, he was unusually irritable, but hadn't yet developed a lot of the physical symptoms. He simply had a runny nose that was slightly yellow. But on this particular day, Jesse was very uncomfortable, rolling around in pain and shoving his hands in his mouth. He wanted to be held, then left alone, then held. I was sure it was an ear infection but when I took him to the doctor, his ears were perfect but his throat was very red. We left without antibiotics. By nightfall, Jesse's eyes were full of green goop and he was miserable. I gave him eye drops before bed, and Tylenol for his throat and possible body aches. In the morning his eyes were glued with goo and his nose was covered with crusty green boogers. My poor kid couldn't see or breathe! But still, it was a viral infection and antibiotics were not needed, other than eye drops. I waited for the ear infection, which generally shows up with any congestion. Thankfully, and surprisingly, the infection never came. Jesse had surgery for ear tubes when he was almost two and the ear infections stayed at bay for several years after.

A cold usually means ear infection, goopy eyes, and a sore throat. It can also include body aches. But a sore throat and body are more difficult to understand because the physical symptoms are hidden. If they are fussier, need more attention than normal, and aren't sleeping as well as they and you are used to, it's likely they are in pain and discomfort. As they get older, about three or four years old, they don't get hit as hard, and generally don't experience the same symptoms. They are also much better at communicating their pain. With older kids you generally won't see as many ear infections or goopy eye problems, but they do still happen.

Common But Random Issues With a Cold

In addition to the above, a virus can also bring on a rash and swollen lymph nodes. The rash can be all over, on just the legs and arms, or isolated to the diaper area. Antibiotics can also cause a yeast like diaper rash. Usually a topical cream specific for yeast can do the trick. If the rash does not come with a fever, or hives (large welt like red spots), it will likely go away and is nothing to worry about. If the rash looks like large welt like bumps, and it comes with a fever, it may be a reaction or infection to something, and you'll want to head to the pediatrician. If it appears during a round of antibiotics, it could be an allergic reaction to the antibiotics.

Swollen lymph nodes can be alarming because they feel like large lumps under the skin. Pay attention to these lumps— when they show up and where they are on the body. If they seem to be more noticeable during an illness and are around the areas where lymph nodes are found, it's very likely they are inflamed or swollen lymph nodes. Initially it may scare you, and this is why it's important to think about how he's been feeling and other signs and symptoms you may have also noticed. If the lump becomes large and noticeable to the eye, there may be an infection. I've had a few experiences with infected lymph nodes, and both times the infected area was on the neck, right below the ear. Joe had just finished antibiotics for a double ear infection and a knot started forming on his neck, just below his ear. It got quite large in just a day and became noticeable. It was close to the size of a golf ball. When I took him in to see his pediatrician, she said it was an infected lymph node. She put him on antibiotics for ten more days!

"When my son was almost two he had severe swelling on one side of his neck. After taking him to the doctor, several unsuccesful antiobiotics, and an ER trip, a CT scan revealed an inflamed cyst in his lymph node. Apparently he was born with it but a virus caused it to swell. I feared the absolute worst but I was SO relieved that it could be treated, and I cried, a ton!"

— Amanda, mother of 2

Sick kids are exhausting and tough to manage. It can be even tougher when they start feeling better because they can get spoiled, and it happens very quickly. All kids need the extra TLC when they are sick. When my kids were very young, they needed a lot more for a lot longer than their illness lasted. It's not always easy to determine if they need you because they are still sick, or if it's because they have gotten used to the attention. Everything learned in their sleep training flies out the window when they are aren't feeling well.

Joe was eleven months old and teething (I think) when he woke up screaming. He screamed for over an hour, while of course, I went in every ten minutes. I gave him Tylenol and changed him and he kept screaming. Finally, after an hour and a half, I brought him into bed with me, and he crashed!

The next night, after a fussy day, I gave him Tylenol and put him to bed. After fussing a little he fell asleep quickly. He woke up two hours later, screaming and for the next several hours I was in and out of sleep, each time waking up to his crying. I wondered if he too had been in and out of sleep, or if he had just never stopped crying. I went in and gave a binkie, and left him crying, again. Eventually, after calming from hysterics and me feeling horrible, he finally went to sleep. I breathed a sigh of relief and went to bed. Of course, then I worried because he was so quiet! And, for some reason (I'm a mom), I worried

What We've Learned As Parents About Illness and Kids:

△ Have a pain reducer AND fever reducer on hand at all times (but read the labels and talk to your pediatrician about how best to use them). We've found that Motrin works best for pain, but we often try not to use either.

△ Have Benadryl or other allergy medication in your collection of kids' medicine.

△ Essential oils can be used for relief of many symptoms from illness.

△ Keep prescription eye and eardrops for future eye and ear gunk. The eye drops will be very helpful when your child gets the glossy, goopy eye. If anything you can use the drops until you get a new prescription, and your child won't wake up with eyes glued shut by goop.

△ Always have eardrops for pain because you'll learn that earaches rarely start during the day. Typically, it starts just as your head hits the pillow.

△ Keep any prescription rash or skin cream for future use.

△ Really bad barking coughs always get better with cold air or steam.

△ Hand, foot, and mouth is a virus that starts with a fever, and involves blisters around the mouth. My kids never had this, but it exists and is very contagious!

△ A fever that lasts needs to be addressed.

△ Unusual pain and irritation that does not seem normal should not be ignored. Trust your gut if you feel something is not right, and go with it.

that I caused him permanent emotional scarring from leaving him in bed, even though I'd done the same thing several times before with the others.

It is always difficult when a child is sick. It adds stress to an already intense situation, and the amount of sleep lost only makes it worse. Have faith that it will pass, and remember to trust your mother's intuition, as it is a very powerful thing.

△ Notes

Eight

Going Back To Work

The first week back to work is extremely difficult. In addition to the separation anxiety many new moms feel from leaving their newborns, many moms experience a great challenge in developing a new relationship with their breast pump. It will be a tough transition. Preparation is imperative to a successful transition out of the home and away from baby.

Preparing You and Your Baby

As you are preparing to go back to work, it is really important to create a pumping and bottle-feeding schedule a few weeks before you return to work. I cannot emphasize this enough. Your body and breasts need to adjust to the supply and demand of a pumping and nursing schedule, and your baby needs to adjust to bottle-feeding. An electronic pump expresses milk slightly different than your baby, and it isn't nearly as efficient. You will find that pumping four ounces may become difficult early on in your return to work. If your body is not used to the reduced demand for milk, it will continue to produce more milk than you can comfortably handle, and your initial return to work will be very uncomfortable, and could lead to breast infections from engorgement. The better prepared you and your body are for the transition, the easier it will be. It took one to two weeks for my breasts to adjust to eliminating a feeding. The emotional stress involved in going back to work will be enough to handle. Adding physical discomfort to the situation might make adjusting to this next chapter feel impossible.

Pumping may be difficult to do at home when you still have time with your baby. And it may be difficult and heartbreaking to stop nursing. It's possible that two weeks may be way too early for you emotionally to start this transition. If this is the case, waiting one more week to start the transition will still be very healthy for you and your baby. I had a difficult time pumping when it meant missing an opportunity to breast-feed. Plus, it's not all that fun to pump. The setup and cleanup involved takes more time and effort than nursing, and obviously when you pump, you miss out on the emotional connection with your baby.

> "Finding the right childcare is essential to feeling good about going back to work. We explored large centers, daycares, nanny shares, and grandparent care. I had no idea what the right childcare would be for us, but I inched closer to a comfort level after visiting six to seven different places."
> — Theresa, mother of 2

It may help to think about how difficult it might be for your baby to transition to a bottle. If you find your baby is having a hard time adjusting, it would be better to discover this with enough time to work with the problem. Introducing a bottle early, at about two weeks, and again at four weeks will help your baby with the transition. If you find he is adjusting just fine to a bottle, starting a week before returning to work should be plenty of time. However, if a bottle just isn't his idea of comfort, he may need more than a week to get used to the idea. Understanding the emotional struggles for you and your baby may make it easier to start early. There's nothing worse than going to work the first day, crying because you miss your baby, and then discovering on your lunch that he hasn't eaten all day because he's not taking to the transition to the bottle. You don't want to be in this situation.

△ **FYI:** *There's nothing worse than going to work the first day, crying because you miss your baby, and then discovering on your lunch that he hasn't eaten all day because he's not taking to the transition to the bottle.*

Recognizing the possible difficulties your baby may face will help you start your transition to work when you feel it's right for both of you.

A Morning Routine

Early to bed is the key. Yeah, right! It's much easier said than done. When you have a six-week-old baby, generally she isn't sleeping on her own, all night, and on command. So, it can be tough to go to bed early and to get enough sleep. The sleep routines and habits you create early on with your baby will help with your workday mornings. Putting your baby to bed at 8pm and having her sleep right away will happen, but it starts with creating a comfortable, safe bedtime routine, and also encouraging peaceful solidarity in her bassinet. What I mean by this is allowing her to cry a little and comfort herself in her own way, without picking her up. Not only will this help at bedtime, but also in the morning when you're trying to get yourself ready for work. Instead of rushing to pick her up when she cries, and facing a generous delay in your departure, you will feel comfortable letting her work it out on her own, and she will be comfortable being left alone for a bit.

As you start back to work your morning routine will be easier if you first get yourself ready. This means getting up early and likely before you're ready, and before baby is ready to eat. If your baby generally wakes up at 5:30 to eat, try to get up at 5:00 to shower. Again, it's easier said than done. Five o' clock comes much sooner than you feel you can handle when you've been up all night taking care of Baby, but waking up before your baby will give you a little time without worrying that she needs you. A baby that is awake, alone, and happy in her bassinet will be the difference between morning meltdowns for mom and baby and a smooth beginning to each day. It is one of the most difficult things, bordering impossible, to stay calm and efficient when you have a screaming child in the background, as you are attempting to get yourself ready. Also, worries like "What if she cries while I'm in the shower?" or "Will I hear her if she cries?," will make it difficult to stay on track. Remember that it is okay to let your baby cry, and

△ **TIP:** *Your morning routine and starting back to work will be easier if you first get yourself ready. This means getting up early and likely before you're ready, and before baby is ready to eat.*

if you're used to it, and she's used to it, allowing her to fuss won't be so tough. It also won't be something you deal with every day.

Imagine how difficult it would be to get yourself ready for a long workday when your baby is screaming nonstop and you can't pick her up. If you do pick her up you'll probably end up being late to work, *every day*. I don't think this would go over well with your employer. At least not after a week or two.

Get yourself ready first. Do as much as you possibly can the night before. For example, pack the diaper bag and your bag the night before. I liked to put the diaper bag on the counter with bottles in sight so I would remember to pack the breast milk from the freezer. When possible, I tried to keep diapering stuff and extra clothing at the daycare so I didn't have to pack every day. You may also be able to keep a large supply of diapers and wipes at your daycare for a month at a time, which is also very helpful.

If you are able to take a shower at night, you will find the transition during your first few weeks much easier. Then again for me, my morning showers are absolutely necessary! Without them I would be a little grumpier and less awake, no question. A shower at night will be one less thing to do in the morning, and if this helps you transition, then do it! At this stage it's important to do what works, even if it seems difficult. Then, when you're completely ready, spend some time with your little one before you head off to work. Having this time, even if it's short, will help you survive each day.

The First Week Back

The first week back to work will be difficult. I cried a whole lot on the way to daycare, from daycare to work, every day. At first I felt that I would be sad forever and that it would be extremely hard to leave her. But it got easier. After a few weeks, my hormones settled down, a routine started forming, my schedules were made, and my life felt manageable. I found this pattern in transitioning with all five of my children.

When at Work

Pumping first thing after arriving to work will help you start your day right. After packing bags, dropping off, and getting to work, you will be physically ready to pump when you arrive. You will want to empty your breasts before starting your workday to avoid feeling uncomfortable and to prevent leakage. Also, if you want to continue to breastfeed, it will help to pump when you get to work, at lunch, and before you head home. This will stimulate demand, and will tell your body to continue producing milk throughout the day even when your baby isn't with you. Otherwise your milk will slowly dry up and you won't have enough to satisfy, which may result in the refusal of the breast and Baby will want the bottle instead.

> "Converting from a working woman to a stay at home mom was a little weird at first. I felt like I wasn't contributing enough or being productive. It's strange being dependent financially on someone else."
>
> — Kara, new mom

Returning to work six weeks, twelve weeks, or any amount of time after having a baby can be difficult for everyone involved. It's even more difficult if Baby is still breastfeeding. It can seem as if it will never get easier. Even though this stage is difficult, planning ahead, transitioning your baby slowly, and having faith that the sadness will end can help. The process will get easier and easier. I promise.

△ Notes

Nine

Stages, Milestones and Other Gems

I'm not going to go through all of the stages to expect and when to expect them. All babies are different, and they hit their milestones at different times. As long as they are progressing, getting to each milestone, and perfecting it, they are doing well. When they are several months behind what is typical, the situation should be evaluated.

What I've included in this chapter are the difficult stages that a lot of new parents ask about, as well as the underlying challenges that show up when your child becomes more active. I'm sure you've noticed that most of what I've written implies that parenting is anything but fun. It's the difficult part of parenting that requires some warning. There are a lot of stages and milestones that bring smiles, laughter, and enjoyment and remind you why you became a parent. I just don't write about many of them in this book.

Teething

Babies start teething at different ages. A few of my babies started teething around six to seven months, and usually cut their first tooth around eight or nine months. Jesse and Joe didn't start teething until almost a year. A good indication of a teething baby is a lot of saliva and chewing. Teething babies often have the urge to chew on anything near their mouth.

They find toys, blankets, their hands or yours, and food. They might also be unusually fussy and have a slight fever. When Joe was approaching his first birthday I wondered if he was teething. His moods were all over the place. He would seem fine and then suddenly cry out. Sometimes he'd shove his hands or his toy in his mouth, and then let loose. This type of crying, in my experience, was most often due to pain. Teething can last for several months, and the extreme fussiness occurs when the tooth is pushing its way through the gum.

Joe's eyeteeth came in around twenty months. This experience is one that is vivid in my mind because it turned my sweet little boy into an intolerable pain in the neck! He screamed. He was grumpy. He wasn't eating well. His mouth seemed swollen and sore. I didn't make the connection until I noticed the tip of his eyetooth poking through his swollen gums while I was changing his diaper. He was screaming in protest so I was able to get a good look. I felt terrible that I hadn't noticed it sooner. I would have been so much more compassionate. I don't remember the other kids reacting so strongly to getting teeth. It's possible that after dealing with five teething children, I finally figured it out.

There are a lot of teething remedies available. I tried many tricks including the teething gel for sore and swollen gums. I tried this only a handful of times and never had great results. Babies produce so much saliva, especially when they are teething. I found that the gel washed away before it could really do much good. The best teething relief for my kids was always Tylenol and a good teething toy. An easy to chew, easy to grab, rubber chew toy seemed to be enough to distract them from the pain. Teethers that can be frozen are also nice. If I didn't have a toy handy I used my finger. This only happened if my hands were fairly clean and I had nothing else. Giving your baby a finger to chew on can also help you "feel out" the situation. If there is a tooth coming through the gum or if the gums are swollen, you may feel it. How hard they bite can also be a good indicator of whether they are in fact teething. As far as Tylenol or other pain reducers, this was and is always used sparingly, and only if their misery keeps them from sleeping. It works wonders but has potential risks and side effects, as does any medication.

Crawling

Crawling is something you wait for as a new parent. It is a very exciting time, and the process can seem to take ages for them to graduate to using both arms and legs together where they actually move forward. The first few months, the crawl looks like an army crawl with arms and elbows pulling the legs behind. You may wonder how long it will take him to start using his knees. It generally takes a few months for the whole body to work together. It takes full body strength, especially the core muscles, to coordinate a full crawl. Early tummy time will really help with developing these muscles. When he does finally crawl on his hands and knees, it starts out as a mix of some hands and knee crawling and some army crawls until full strength is developed.

Crawling is very important for hand and eye coordination. It's helpful to encourage crawling by modeling and helping them to feel the motion. Some babies skip the crawling stage altogether. If you have any control, help them develop the crawl before the walk. When they show an interest in moving, you can help motivate them with toys or interesting things. When they play on their tummies, place toys just beyond their reach and encourage them to push with their feet to move closer to the object. This practice will help develop the army crawl that will eventually turn into the real thing. It will also help you train for chasing down little movers! If they take the baby steps to walking by scooting or doing the army crawl, you'll be better prepared for the walking, running, and climbing. It's easier to chase a crawling baby than a baby that runs. This slow transition will better prepare you for the next milestones.

It's very exciting when your baby starts showing physical strength and motivation for crawling. New parents, however, don't realize that with the crawling comes the scary, frustrating, and very time-consuming stage of "everything in the mouth." When our last guy started crawling, I wasn't ready to combat the constant hand to mouth activity, which usually involved pieces of crayon, rubber bands, and leftovers from

△ **FYI:** *New parents don't realize that with the crawling comes the scary, frustrating, and very time-consuming stage of "everything in the mouth."*

the meal before. EVERYTHING goes in the mouth, so it's important and helpful that you:

△ Watch him very carefully if he is roaming free. Keeping a close eye on a baby can be hard to do if you have other kids and are busy or distracted.

△ Have a "cage" to put him in when you have an enticing leftover of food or Legos that haven't yet been cleaned up. A gated area works wonders for this.

△ Get a baby's eye view of the floor by crawling around and checking for choking hazards. Rubber bands and hair ties are tough to see so an army crawl is even more effective in locating small objects. Trust me on this one—they will always find what you don't.

△ Keep your floor immaculate so there is very little chance he will find something to eat. When you have older kids, this can be difficult.

△ Have the little guy help you clean because he *will* find what you did not. If you can believe it, mobile babies are better at picking up than vacuum cleaners.

A scary example of this happened when Joe was ten months old. Our family took a weekend vacation to the coast and stayed in a hotel. We stayed one night, and that night before going to bed my husband dropped a pill while trying to put the lid back on the bottle. The pill was smaller than a Tic Tac, and we knew we needed to find it. We looked for twenty minutes crawling on the floor, even going as far as resting our heads on the floor to really get an eye-level view. We found nothing and went to bed. In the morning we woke up and looked a little more with no luck. We were afraid to put Joe on the floor because we knew he would find the pill and put it straight to his mouth. We *needed* to find it, so we put him down and watched. Within five minutes he found it, and wouldn't you know, I turned my head for about thirty seconds and looked back just in time to see his fingers coming out of his mouth. By the time I got to him, the pill had nearly dissolved in his mouth. Needless to say, we took him to the ER when we got home. He was okay.

It's not always a pill or something dangerous that goes in the mouth when a baby starts moving. A month later we took our first real weeklong family vacation to the beach. We had plans to spend a lot of time on the beach, building sandcastles and jumping waves. It was our first time at the beach with a crawler and we weren't thinking much about containing him. We weren't worried about him eating things off the floor because there wouldn't be a floor for finding things. You might assume we would be smarter than this, having had a lot of experience with curious crawlers, but Jesse missed this stage so we had forgotten some of the risks.

We took the five-minute walk down to the beach with Jesse and Joe in our jogging stroller, the other three walking alongside us. When we found our spot in the sand we set up camp, rolled out the blanket, and unpacked our sand castle tools. Within two minutes, Joe had crawled from the middle of the blanket to the edge and stuck a fistful of sand into his mouth. We caught him just as he was reaching for another fistful. What was he thinking? He seemed to like it because he kept reaching for more. Now, ingested sand is not all that dangerous, but it can be a pain when it finally comes out. It's bad enough changing a diaper full of poop, but the mess is much worse when it is a diaper full of sandy poop.

Walking, Running and Climbing

One of the most exciting baby milestones is walking. When walking becomes the new skill to practice, it seems that your baby is graduating from baby to toddler. As with crawling, the faster mobility of walking has its pitfalls. A faster toddler to chase after is a big challenge, along with harder and farther falls.

Babies have been known to walk as early as seven to eight months, but most babies will start their first steps between ten and fifteen months of age. Ryanne started walking at almost eleven months. Reese was about thirteen months. Jack was very similar to Reese at about twelve to thirteen months. Jesse walked at two years, and we were thrilled! Joe took his first steps right at twelve months. First steps typically happen after a baby has been "cruising" the couch or other furniture.

When they feel strong enough and confident to let go, they do. Some babies take their first steps and are walking within a few days. Others take longer to progress. You can expect that most babies new to walking will be pretty unsteady on their feet. They will fall a lot, and in every direction you can think of—forwards, backwards, sideways. When you have a rookie walker it can be helpful to:

△ Move sharp furniture out of the way.

△ Move anything that can tip or roll, because a new walker will try to pull up to a stand using anything she can reach. An unsteady chair will tip over if it's pulled. Wheels will roll if they are pushed, and baby will go down with whatever she is holding.

△ Barefoot is best or shoes that are very soft soled, like Robeez® or other similar brands. Babies use their toes to help keep their balance, and it's much easier to do this when they can feel and "grab" the floor.

△ Keep loose items near the walls or off the floor completely. Babies tend to trip on everything when they are first learning to walk.

> **"My kids ALL walked before eleven months old, but this was before swings, jumpers and walkers, and my kids spent a lot more time on the floor, rolling and moving."**
>
> **— Leslie, veteran mother of 6**

By the time babies start running, they are very steady walkers, and they generally know their safe speed limit. Sometimes they do try to run faster than their legs can take them, and they may fall or trip on something. Climbing, however, is much worse than crawling, walking or running. Their first attempt at climbing starts with the couch, which isn't that big of a deal. When they start climbing the counter stools that sit thirty inches above porcelain tile, it's scary. For some reason they know they shouldn't climb them, and this is why they do.

Once my kids made it to the top of the tall chair and saw how scared and anxious I became, it was their mission to climb the tall chair every time they had the chance. There is not much you can do about this attitude. I discovered that if I was consistent and grabbed them before or as they were climbing, and told them, "No, no—that's not safe," they eventually stopped trying, but it took several months.

Climbers are fearless! They will climb up, down and all around anything they can reach. They don't always understand their spatial surroundings and can still fall off couches, beds, slides, or anything with an edge. If possible, stage a fall for them where it is safe, soft, and low, so they can feel the fall but not get hurt. Joe had a terrible fall from a counter stool when he was a toddler. He made it to the top without a problem, but somehow he managed to tip the stool just enough, and he went down with the chair. He crashed into the wall first, saving his head from hitting the tile, but the impact of landing made him bite his lip. The result—a trip to the ER, three stitches in his lip and a scar that may never go away.

Stages and Milestones of a One-Year-Old

Mimicking is a fun stage most of the time, that starts around the age of one, and can remain an obvious behavior until they turn two, or longer. Typically around this time they become copycats and do and say just what you do, sometimes right away, and other times later. Sometimes it's cute and an acceptable behavior, so laughing is expected. Other times it's imitating a back talk or disciplining behavior. Joe started giving it back when we would tell him no, or when his brother Jesse would bug him. He would point his finger, scrunch up his nose and lips, and give the what for, almost like he was scolding everyone. It was very cute, but we tried hard not to smile or laugh because it only encouraged him to do it more. Talking back and scolding Mom and Dad was never allowed, even when it came from an unsuspecting toddler, so we ignored the behavior and tried not to laugh.

When babies reach the age of mimicking, it's a good idea to watch your words and behavior. It's amazing how precise kids can be at reenacting your own tantrums or repeating adult vocabulary using the same inflection and tone as you used. I have often wondered about my own behavior, sometimes even questioning it when I see my little ones doing what I do, or becoming a little version of me as they get older. They will grow up to be versions of you so it's important to model good behavior and an appropriate use of vocabulary. Sometimes this can be difficult, especially if you used colorful language before Baby.

Stranger Anxiety

Stranger anxiety begins around the age of one. Sometimes it starts sooner. Babies can get very shy. They may put their head down or avoid eye contact. Most babies go through a stranger anxiety period, however, their personality will determine how severe it is and how long it lasts. This behavior can happen around nine to twelve months. They may look to you for approval if a stranger talks to them. They may cry or may turn away. I was always so ready for a break that I usually just ignored their protest and handed them over. The stranger, of course, was always a close family member who was a stranger to the baby but not a stranger to anyone else. If you allow the child to be afraid and shy, it will be more difficult for her to warm up to people, and she will struggle more often when she is away from Mom and Dad.

Ryanne was very confident and never seemed bothered by a lot of people and strangers. Joe, on the other hand, was very shy and skeptical for about a year. All of our kids had their moments, and shied away from strangers a little. Overall, we really tried to encourage them to feel comfortable with people. We never avoided large gatherings with our kids and gladly handed them off to someone wanting and willing to take them.

One-year-olds are smart. Don't underestimate the intellectual capabilities of your newly walking, newly talking little person. They understand how to manipulate. They get jealous if someone else is getting what they want, whether it's extra attention from mom or maybe a special toy. They are great at throwing "mini" tantrums. The "mini" tantrum just implies that the tantrums get bigger as kids get bigger. NIP IT EARLY! One-year-olds understand cause and effect, and they know that if they scream and get a toy, they can scream every time and

△ **FYI:** *One-year-olds are great at throwing "mini" tantrums when they are unhappy or want something. I say "mini" because their tantrums become much bigger as they get bigger. NIP IT EARLY!*

will be rewarded. Kicking, screaming, and head throwing are all great weapons for them, and they know it. If you are holding one of these crazy kids when a tantrum occurs, hold on tight so she doesn't fly out of your grasp. Take a deep breath or two, and count to ten—gently lay her on the floor, carpet, or concrete, and let her finish the fit. It's important to breathe and pause *before* laying her down, or the "gently" part might not happen. The one-year-old tantrums usually stop quickly once they realize they might hurt themselves if they keep it up. Establish early that the fits are powerless, or their fits will get worse and more difficult to control. The terrible twos may become more than just terrible.

The Terrible Twos

Many experts debate when the so-called terrible twos take hold. Or maybe there is no debate and I just disagree with the age of two. For us, for the most part, all of that lovely behavior hit earlier than the age of two, around eighteen months. Imagine a possessed child, screaming and head flipping around in protest. Sometimes there is an intentional fall or throw down to the ground. This moment of insanity happens any time he doesn't get what he wants. For Joe this behavior started from his obsession with the iPad. At almost two years old, he had learned to successfully navigate the games, audio books, and episodes of *The Backyardigans*. When he wanted to play and didn't get to, he would do all of the above, and it would last for an hour. Then he'd get really needy and want to be picked up. To this reaction I have always said, and still say, *let them throw their fit!* In my experience, as soon as the fit starts, I carefully and gently move them to a safe place and lower them down on to a soft surface, (if they aren't already down) and I walk away. I ignore them. Eventually they learn to stop soon after they start. If not the first time, or the second or third time, they will soon understand that the meltdown doesn't get them anywhere, and hopefully will decide against the fit.

I often wondered about my kids—*Where did they learn that this reaction would work?* Tantrums were never acknowledged, yet they still happened, even as they got older. Joe seemed to be the worst! It is possible I just don't remember the other kids

△ *In my experience, as soon as the fit starts, I carefully and gently move them to a safe place and lower them down on to a soft surface, if they aren't already down, and I walk away. I ignore them.*

because I've blocked them out. Joe would scream as if his hand had been cut off if I tried to put him in the car, or if I brought him inside after spending hours playing outside. If I tried to put him in his high chair when he didn't want to be in it, he would almost fly out of my arms if I wasn't holding on tight. I truly believe it's the age. If I do remember correctly, it goes away or lessens dramatically when they reach age two. The behavior of course, comes back around three, and again at almost four.

At three and a half, Joe started to test his limits again. His fits came back in redundant spurts of screaming bloody murder, for no apparent reason. He started speaking defiantly to us when we expected something from him. He even started getting into trouble at school for not listening. It was a rough period, but short-lived. He eased out of this stage after a few months and entered the wonderful stage of pleasing. Sigh.

> "When my daughter was three she was adamant about not showering with me. She refused, several times, to get undressed so I put her in the shower fully clothed, in her favorite blue dress for that matter. She was not happy."
>
> — Rebecca, veteran mother of 3

Diaper changes get really tough around seventeen to eighteen months. They kick, scream, roll, turn, or do anything to get away. I've tried everything, even trapping them with my legs, but the most successful strategy was the art of distraction. When my kids went though this stage, I used to distract them with nearby toys. It was usually a cell phone, TV remote, or some grown-up toy that worked the best for keeping them occupied. Counting is also very distracting and has worked well for me. If they understand counting in English and Spanish, you might have twice as much time to change the diaper! It's important to give the toy *before* the fit, otherwise it seems like he's getting a reward or something extra for screaming and kicking. You can also take the toy away if he starts up again. These attempts at escaping only lasted a month with Joe, and he started cooperating again.

Behavior stages fluctuate so much during the ages of one to five. They throw mini tantrums that turn into big tantrums when they get close to age three or a little beyond. The most difficult behavior and the one I would really characterize as "terrible," occurs from the age of three and a half to four and a half. During this stage, my kids threw fits, knowing they were pointless. It's as if they tried testing all over again. They tested everything from naptime to bedtime. They even *forgot* how to stay in their room when they made a bad choice. I discussed this in an earlier chapter when I described the sleeping habits of Jack. His decision to quit naps altogether and to quit sleeping in his own bed was an attempt at redefining his boundaries. During this difficult age, it seems that everything they do is the opposite of what you ask. If they have choices to make, they seem to make the wrong choice nine out of ten times. My kids' interactions with their dad and I were more like moments of irritation and disrespect. It is a frustrating stage, but it will pass. When it does pass they become pleasant and endearing. At around age four, your sweet child should come back to you, wanting to please and make you happy and proud. This is a great time to create opportunities for him to be proud of himself, too.

△ **FYI:** *The most difficult behavior and the one I would really characterize as "terrible," occurs from the age of three and a half to four and a half.*

"The paci battle was some of our most epic. We have the negotiator on our hands and I've lost track of all the tantrums."
— Erin, mother of 2

You can expect a lot of changes in behavior as they grow. When they are at the age of starting kindergarten or are already in their first year of school, you may notice a change in how they act. In their first few months of kindergarten they may be very tired and mentally drained. This exhaustion tends to influence whining and complaining, and the smallest issue can become an enormous problem.

Beyond their first year in kindergarten, they begin to adjust to life and are better able to control their fits and sometimes their moods. Also remember that personalities and physical needs can bring on mood swings and difficult behavior. It may be that a small snack is needed to level out blood sugar and mood. We have found that when our children are in need of sustenance and energy, they become very agitated. Ryanne has been the most affected by low blood sugar and we notice this need even now. Once we realized this, we were better able to control her moods with food. As they get older, it's easier to notice patterns in behavior, and they can communicate what they feel or what they need. However, the tantrums still exist with older children, and it can be much more difficult to handle these episodes.

> **"I asked my daughter to put her dirty clothes in the laundry basket—total meltdown as she went up the stairs! She screamed at us that 'she is just the Cinderella of this family!'"**
>
> — Wendy, mother of 3

Outings With Littles

We have always felt confident when taking our kids to restaurants or the grocery store because, in general, they understand their boundaries. If they are ever angry at us or disagree with the situation, they rarely voice their opinions in public, or at least not loud enough to make a scene. They accept "no" as an answer and generally handle it calmly. It is rare that I leave a full cart of groceries, dragging a possessed child along the floor or carrying him in my arms because of a tantrum. The only problem I can recall when taking the kids to a supermarket was fitting anything in the cart because the kids took up all the cart space. Also, the fighting, that frankly still happens among all of them, has sometimes been enough to leave.

Although difficult, we can all usually get through an outing without any major mishaps. I have to bribe them or threaten the loss of a privilege, but this tactic works pretty well. I won't lie. After years of taking kids to the store, we had our first real dramatic moment when Jack was five. It wasn't a tantrum or fighting, but the situation caused a scene.

I had all five at the grocery store and the older three were taking turns pushing the little ones in the cart. It was Jack's turn to steer the cart, and he was doing a great job missing customers and displays until...he forgot to look forward while he was pushing and he ran straight into an allergy medication display. He knocked the whole thing down and boxes of Claritin flew in every direction, as far as they could possibly travel. It was a mess, to say the least, and my first real embarrassing moment as a parent in a grocery store. We cleaned it up as quickly as possible and headed straight for check out. Thankfully we were finished shopping.

> "'Eyes only' is one of the best tips I heard from someone else to teach my daughter to look with her eyes in stores, instead of her hands. I used it as a prompt when she went toward unsafe things and it was much better than firmly telling her 'no' or 'don't touch'. It was much more positive."
>
> — Monica, mother of 2

How you handle fits and the consistency of your discipline strategies will teach your kids how serious you are about allowing bad behavior or whether you will be giving consequences when the behavior happens. If they understand your expectations, and you teach them early, going out in public with your family should be pleasant and not something you try to avoid.

> "Do not worry about the judgment of others, when dealing with a fit in public. They are either glad it's not their kid, or they probably don't have children. Their opinion doesn't matter, anyway. I mean, like they haven't had their child throw one or been a child who threw one themselves."
>
> — Ashlie, mother of 2

Talking

Speech develops at different times for all kids. All of my kids started talking at very different ages. Ryanne and Jack were early talkers and were saying short sentences at eighteen months. Reese and Joe only *started* their output of language around eighteen months. Jesse still struggles with oral communication and he is seven years old, although his verbal communication is improving quickly. Most of the time, the reason for early speech development or delay is unknown and generally isn't an issue until they are around the age of three. If they are not talking by age three, the concern needs to be addressed. The delay may not be for any reason, but early intervention is best.

> "The general rule of the thumb for language development is that a child's sentence length should correspond with his age. For example, a two-year-old child should have a MLU (mean length utterance), or average sentence length of two words. A three-year-old should have a MLU of three words, and so on."
>
> — Dawn Bereznak, SLP M.A.

△ **FYI:** *The most successful way to influence speech output is with a lot of input and repetition.*

As their speech develops, you may notice that sometimes the pronunciation of words or specific letters is incorrect or incomplete. Typical first words include up, down, out, more, all done, please, thank you, mama, dada, ball, oh no, uh oh, milk, juice (without the c) it's really neat to be able to communicate with them once they start attempting it. When Joe was almost two, he started adding a *t* to *out* and a *c* to *juice* and an *s* to *please*. He didn't say sentences, but we felt confident that his speech was developing as expected. At four, his language continued to develop. Now at five, he is communicating very well and with great inflection and personality I might add.

Specific letters can be difficult to say when speech is developing. Our son Jack struggled with pronouncing the *r* and the *s* in his words until he was seven. These are common letters that sometimes take several years to perfect. We were not worried and did not feel an intervention was necessary. He eventually figured it out on his own.

"According to Sanders Norms, the only sounds we expect a three-year-old to be able to produce correctly are the 'p, m, h, n, and w'. Once the child is four we would also like them to be able to produce the 'b, d, t, k and g'."

— Dawn Bereznak, SLP M.A.

If early speech is something you hope for, or want to try to control, there are ways to encourage the process. The most successful way to influence speech output is input and repetition. As a language teacher, my focus is always to give as much input to my students in the most natural way, while trying to repeat key vocabulary. I've tried to do this with my kids. I repeat key words like want, need, have and then emphasize the pronunciation of words in the conversation. As a new parent, I did not understand language like I do now and didn't focus my attention on input and repetition. With Joe, I tried to narrate every move and interaction between us. For example, when I put on his shoes, I would say *shoes and socks* and *on* or *off* several times each time we put shoes on and took them off. It's fun to have a "conversation" with them in sounds and expressions, even if you don't know what the conversation is about. Repeating the sounds he makes and creating a conversation will encourage communication. Jesse has been going to speech therapy for the past few years and will likely continue for several years. What we've learned is that emphasizing expressive language like *uh oh*, *wow*, *oh no*, *yay*, and really playing up words like *up*, *down*, *eat* will improve language tremendously. However, as I mentioned above, giving your child a lot of input and repeating often is essential for language output. It may take some time before your child says much, but it will happen.

△ *"'R' sounds are generally not expected to be mastered until six years of age, while 'S' sounds are typically not mastered until eight years of age, according to Sander's Norms."*

— E. Sander 1972, "When are Speech Sounds Learned?" Journal of Speech and Hearing Disorders

Potty Training

Potty training is not always the easiest solution to diapers. For example, taking a child to the bathroom three times during a Costco trip, only to experience two false alarms and an accident, can be frustrating. Your children know they can play you. They know if they say poop or potty you'll rush them to the bathroom. Sometimes they go, but if they're not ready, most of the time they don't. They know they have to go but haven't yet made the connection of having the need and going in the toilet. This is how it happened for me, and I often regretted trying to train my kids too soon.

Before true readiness occurs, you will get a lot of "crying wolf." For example at bedtime it was "Mama, I have to go potty" and during time out, "Mama, I have to go poo poo." For us, we were very strict with bedtime and time out. Our kids weren't allowed to leave their beds or the timeout spot unless we gave them permission, but "crying poop" changed everything. We were excited that they wanted to go potty but even more afraid they would go in their pants. When they warned us that they had to go, we took it seriously and had a hard time saying no.

In our beginning years of potty training, we fell for the cry every time. "Okay," we'd always say, as we took our sweet little girl to the potty during time out. She'd sit, and sit, and sit until we'd ask her if she really had to go. Of course, she would say, "No, I'm done."

With each of our children, we experienced similar situations at all stages of potty training. All of our children are very different, and the stages varied slightly with ages and enthusiasm, however, with each of them we faced similar milestones and setbacks. When Reese was almost two, at the end of summer, I thought, *Maybe she'll be as quick and easy as her older sister*, who trained herself at twenty-three months, so I pushed her gently into potty training. This, of course, was after she had shown an interest and had gone in the potty a few times already. Instead of pull-ups I used underwear. I let her run around outside, hoping that if and when she peed, she wouldn't like the feeling and would notice the difference. With her sister, the "underwear strategy" worked, and she had only a few accidents and decided she was ready to be a big girl. Like I said, Ryanne wasn't quite two-years-old when she was trained. She didn't even wear pull-ups at night after the first few months! Reese, however, didn't seem to have the same ambition. She didn't notice, or care, that she had wet pants and pee running down her leg. Even after several changes of underwear and hose showers, Reese didn't really understand the goal. I tried a second strategy, (one I had used with Ryanne) and let Reese run through the house footloose and panty-free. Maybe, I thought, the air will feel different, and she'll run to the bathroom if she has to go, because of course, this worked well for Ryanne.

This is when I learned something extremely important about parenting. While cooking in her mini kitchen in the carpeted living room, (as she did often), Reese decided she needed to poop. Now, obviously she didn't head to the toilet or I wouldn't have included this part in my book. It's such a great story I just had to share it! So poop she did, loosely, and all over the carpet. This scenario went from bad to worse because she didn't notice. She continued walking back and forth from her kitchen to her store, stepping on and tracking poop in little footprints all over the house.

Was it right for me to get angry or upset with her? Of course not, and I tried very hard to keep my cool. After all, it was totally my fault I had poop all over my floor. Was it difficult not to get upset with her? Extremely! Especially as I crawled around the floor, soaking, scrubbing, and yes, smelling the carpet for poop spots. I managed to keep my rage inside, thankfully! Had I yelled or been upset with her, it would have caused her shame, embarrassment, and confusion. No doubt she would have connected these feelings with going potty, and this may have negatively affected her idea about going in the toilet.

This taught me a basic rule about parenting: Don't push your children before they are ready. As parents, there are some things you can control and some things you can't. *When* your child is ready to use the potty is something you cannot control, and it might be a mistake to try. Kids will do what they need to do when they are ready, and it's important for us as parents to be aware of their readiness and be extremely supportive throughout these stages.

△ **FYI:** *As parents, there are some things you can control and some things you can't. When your child is ready to use the potty is something you cannot control, and it might be a mistake to try.*

I gave up the potty training with Reese after two days and didn't think of it again until six months later when she came to me wanting to use the potty. She was two and a half and was consistently accident free three weeks later.

> **"Every kid learns to use the potty at some point, so I tried not to make myself crazy over it."**
>
> — Loni, veteran mother of 4

My experience with Reese's potty training validated my decision to back off and let her initiate her own training. Really, it shouldn't be called training but more like potty practice. It needs to be encouraged but not pushed or forced on them, even when you know they are smart enough and ready. It could be that your little two-year-old is so smart, he's purposely NOT going on the potty because he doesn't want someone telling him what to do! It's unlikely this is actually the reason, but there is something in his little mind that is telling him it's still ok to go, and he's just not ready.

It generally isn't helpful to push, force, scold, yell, or do anything else that might discourage your child when potty practice is happening. It will only make them hold on tighter to what keeps them comfortable. It's difficult to change a way of life, and for them the convenience of "just going" has become their way of life. Some may not want to change and will refuse. They will be angry about going, and become deliberate in not cooperating. Not to mention, you, as the parent, will no doubt suffer extreme frustration if you try to push them. However, if they are at potty practicing age, it's helpful to ask and continue asking them if they need or want to use the potty. If our question was *Do you want to go potty*, and the response was, *no*, we responded with a simple, okay. We then encouraged them to let us know when they were ready so we could help them if they needed. We respected their response, but we were consistent in asking. For guidance, here are some stages that I went through with my kids.

Potty Training Stages

△ **First stage:** They became interested in the potty, and started to sit on the toilet.

△ **Second stage:** They had gone a few times on the potty, and were sort of interested, but not that much.

△ **Third stage:** They got excited when they needed to go, but wouldn't go if they didn't want to!

△ **Fourth stage:** They wanted to go, and consciously made an effort to go whenever they felt the need. They asked to go while shopping, in the car, in bed, outside...

In general, and what we experienced with most of our children, the first stage is a developing interest in the potty, and they began to sit on the toilet. Sometimes they were fully clothed and other times they had very little clothing if any. On the rare occasion they would take off everything from the waist down, however, we saw more of this as they got into the second and third stages of practice.

The second stage brings out their independence a little more. This is the stage where they have gone a few times on the potty, and are sort of interested, but not that much. If we asked them about practicing, their usual response was "no," however if potty practice was initiated by them, they were more than happy to try. It was hit or miss, literally, whether they actually made something happen, or even got it in the toilet. The exciting thing is that their interest increases in this stage.

Stage three included much more excitement when they needed to go, but again they were often indifferent on following through. They started going on the potty more often, but would not go if they didn't want to. This is the stage that became much more frustrating for us. We had a difficult time staying patient, knowing they were fully capable and aware of using the toilet. Again, we knew we couldn't make them go if they didn't want to.

The fourth and final stage can take a few weeks to master, or it may take some kids much longer. Within a month of entering stage four, our kids were using the potty consistently, with very little reminding from us. I believe this rapid progress was directly related to their readiness and our willingness to let them decide when (within reason), and also the positivity and encouragement we provided, even when we were frustrated. As they mastered this stage they were consciously making an effort to go whenever they felt the need. Our kids started requesting the potty while shopping, in the car, in bed, outside. It is a great stage to reach, but it can be an adjustment when your usual two-hour errand run turns into three or longer given the extra time needed for all the potty breaks. There will be a lot of stops in the beginning of this fourth stage.

Only time will tell how long you'll spend in each of these stages. A lot of the training or potty practice success depends on the personality of the child. Some kids are ready and fully trained in two weeks, like my girls, and some take a few months, like Jack. Some may even need longer than a few months. Your child will be successful, and when he is, let him know it! Praise him, give high fives, jump up and down screaming from excitement. He needs to know how cool it is that he is using the toilet.

We encouraged using the toilet with rewards. We often used M&Ms or Reese's Pieces as a reward. I gave one M&M for peeing in the potty, and two M&Ms for poop. Any incentive is worth a try. Be careful what and how much you give for each "duty." It's important to pay a reasonable price for potty practice and successes. Otherwise, if you're not careful, you'll be giving a king-sized pack of M&M's a day. Not to mention if you overdo it from the beginning she will probably expect a lot of M&M's each time she goes, no matter how much she does actually go in the potty.

Technology can also be a very good motivator for going, or for even just sitting on the toilet. This is what worked for Joe, thankfully, because we were at a loss with him. When he was a few months away from his third birthday, he hadn't shown any interest in the toilet at all! It was the beginning of summer so I imagined him running outside naked, peeing on the grass, maybe pooping here and there. My vision was very different from how it actually went down. Joe would NOT run around naked! He was very much against going commando, or having his pants, diaper or anything off completely. He would not sit on the toilet! Every time we tried to get him to sit he screamed bloody murder, as if we had cut off his hand. Anything related to nudity and sitting sparked protest and he wouldn't do it! His reaction was even a little funny as he ran around slapping his little penis, acting like it was going to bite him! It was obvious he did not like being exposed. He actually covered himself with his hands, while screaming, crying, and running around like a lunatic.

I was convinced we'd go crazy before getting him to sit on the toilet. He wouldn't do it for candy he wouldn't do it for anything—until I brought out the iPad. I told him he could play on the iPad *as long as* he was sitting on the toilet. He wrestled with me for a minute while I helped get his pants down, but as soon as they were off, he sat and asked for the IPad. Granted, he sat on the potty for more than twenty minutes the first few times with no production, but finally he had success! We screamed and jumped for joy and gave him an M&M. A few repetitions of this, and the iPad became less and less of a motivator, and it was all about the M&Ms for actually going. He was trained in a few weeks.

Joe was at an age where we felt it was time to give him a little nudge, and we had no idea he would react this way. This is how it works with potty practice. Just as it is with so many other stages and milestones of parenting, potty practice also brings a very unpredictable situation. *When* they will be ready, how long it will take them and how frustrating it will be for you are challenges that will only present themselves when you approach the stage. However, staying positive and allowing them to determine the beginning and end of their potty practice will reduce and possibly eliminate a lot of unnecessary frustration for both you and your child.

△ Notes

Ten

Beyond the Typical Illness

Parenting and raising children comes with pressure, worry, and heartache. Imagine having these times ten when you have a child with health problems or special needs. I can't speak for the thousands, if not millions, of parents who have children with special needs, but I can talk about our personal experiences with our boys.

Jesse's Struggles

Jesse's struggles started from birth. When he was a newborn, he slept all the time. I mean *all the time*. He never woke up to feed, he never cried, and he rarely opened his eyes. For a newborn this was not normal, and I knew something wasn't right, but, I didn't know what was wrong. He struggled with eating, gaining weight, low muscle tone, and constipation, but the severity of all of it was yet to be discovered.

When Jesse was seven months old, he had eye surgery to correct Exotropia (outward turned eyes). At this point, we were still unsure how well he could see, because he had not shown a lot of visual potential. We were hoping that this surgery would improve his vision and create a strong visual connection to his brain, which had been the diagnosed problem for his weak visual development. This was a two-hour surgery with general anesthesia, and it was our first time with surgery.

A few months later, Jesse had an MRI, which again required general anesthesia because he was so little and needed to be perfectly still for a long period of time. It was a little easier this time, but the soon-to-come diagnoses and prognoses made it more difficult. Although the MRI did not show anything other than delayed brain development and maturity, we were still very far from knowing and understanding the reason for all of Jesse's delays and medical issues.

For several months after Jesse's MRI, we had very little information but a tremendous amount of worry. At a year old, he still wasn't eating well or gaining weight like a typical one-year-old. He didn't have much of an appetite, and he continued to struggle with eating issues like constant gagging and a complete disinterest in anything going into his mouth.

A few weeks after his first birthday, Jesse had a swallow study done, identifying a swallowing disorder called oral dysphagia. More specifically, his pharyngeal restrictor muscles (the muscles that help move food from the back of the tongue and down the throat) weren't working. This weakness in his swallowing caused a severe gag reflex, hence, the reason for gagging on everything. It also caused an increased risk for aspiration, which occurs when fluid gets into the lungs during the swallowing process. Aspiration can be extremely dangerous if it happens often and in large amounts. Fortunately, Jesse did not show large amounts of aspiration and had never had problems with fluid in his lungs or any other respiratory issues. This did, however, explain why he didn't drink well from a bottle.

We adjusted his positioning during feeding, changed bottle shapes, cut y-shapes in the nipples, and started him on a special, thicker formula. Children with swallowing difficulties have a hard time with liquids that are too thin, like water or juice, and foods or liquids that are too thick. His new formula was a safer, thicker consistency with double the calories of regular formula. Although we saw a slight improvement with his intake of formula by bottle, we still struggled with his lack of desire to eat. He never seemed hungry.

My motherly instincts told me something was not right with his swallowing. I had very strong feelings that he had throat pain, or some other issue, but never persisted in finding out.

I felt confident that the professionals would figure it out, but it wasn't the doctors who discovered it. It was his therapists— the other people in his life who worked closely with him. They had a feeling, and they acted on it, which is what I should have done early on but didn't trust my instincts enough to pursue them. Once again, I found myself at the same place: instincts that something else was going on but no direction. My intuition continued to haunt me with thoughts of another, underlying problem.

As we started the sick season of winter and continued into spring Jesse got sick more times than I've ever seen a kid get sick. He had ear infection after ear infection, with at least six infections in four months. He had the stomach flu four times with vomiting and diarrhea, a lovely gift from his siblings no doubt. But in between all of this, he had other pain and vomiting episodes. He would get sick when no one else was. He would have obvious pain, somewhere in his midsection, and then spend most of the night vomiting and feeling extremely uncomfortable. We took him to the emergency room four times from February to May because of pain, vomiting, lack of appetite, and lethargy. One time specifically I remember him twisting in pain and holding what looked like his kidneys. He was arching his back and screaming. My instinct told me that his kidneys were bothering him. I mentioned this to the nurse when we finally got to a room. I also mentioned this to the ER doctor, who basically told me that arching his back is a normal sign of reflux in babies. When his urine sample came back normal, I temporarily dismissed my concern with his kidneys and waited for him to feel better.

In a fluke discovery, while checking his liver in an abdominal sonogram, we finally had something. *Why were we checking his liver?* In several blood tests performed from January to June, his liver enzymes were showing very high levels. Our pediatrician wanted to investigate the cause of his high liver enzymes, so she ordered an abdominal sonogram. In the sonogram his liver looked completely normal, but his kidneys were showing abnormal shaping and size with severe enlargement. A referral to his urologists and a special X-ray test showed that Jesse had what's called Hydronephrosis. More specifically, a Ureteropelvic Junction or UPJ obstruction (partial blockage of the kidney), which was causing severe kidney dilation and very likely the source of the pain and vomiting he was experiencing.

A diagnosis, finally! It's hard to explain the relief we all felt at having a possible answer to Jesse's problems. It wasn't great news because it would require kidney surgery. But it was an answer. When I got home I looked online and, sure enough, found out that most of Jesse's physical symptoms pointed to hydronephrosis. We were one step closer to an answer. Jesse was scheduled to have kidney surgery five weeks later, and it couldn't have come any sooner.

Jesse had his worst episode five days before his surgery. He was irritable for four days, not wanting to eat much. He was very fussy and very uncomfortable. On day five of his episode, two days before his surgery, Jesse started the vomiting. He threw up six times from 2pm to 7pm. He cried, twisted in pain, and cried more. He finally fell asleep, putting an end to yet another horrible episode. Two days later, we drove down to UC Davis for his surgery. What the urologist found during surgery was even better than just the surgery itself. The urologist discovered two crossing blood vessels at the obstruction site. What this meant was that Jesse's pain and vomiting was most definitely caused by the obstruction and the crossing blood vessels. It was great news for all of us! Only time would tell if the surgery had fixed the problem. A few months after his surgery, Jesse's episodes were much fewer and further between, although still an issue. After a second surgery a year later on his left kidney, the issue was fixed! His appetite increased, and his weight started improving. We were finally at a point where we could focus more on his eating and work with the feeding issues that had been building since his birth.

Feeding Difficulties

I will avoid going into great detail on his feeding issues or the feeding therapy he's been doing for several years, but I will share a little of what I believe may help some mothers or parents who struggle with picky eaters. When babies and young toddlers are first learning to feed, the important thing is to identify and show the child who is in charge at feeding time.

Establish who's in charge early. When a baby or child starts to become resistant to eating, or eating a certain type of food, it's important that this behavior is stopped quickly. My advice, as I've been through a ton of feeding experiences with Jesse, is to teach compliance early. What this means is that when you ask him to take a bite of something, whether you are holding the spoon or he is, he must take the bite. You will never be able to force him to eat something, but you can teach him how to do what you ask by providing lots of praise and rewards for complying with a request.

To teach compliance, begin with food that they like. Ask them to take a bite and tell them they can have X when they take their bite. Stay positive and hold out until they comply with your request. Once they understand what the expectations are and what they need to do, you can start introducing non-preferred foods. However, introduce these non-preferred foods slowly, and start with a very small amount. It needs to be something they can accomplish without getting tired or frustrated easily. For example, if they see a large portion of green food they know they don't like, they may get defeated before even beginning. Every time they take a bite, or take three bites, or whatever it is that you are asking them to do, reward them with a preferred toy or maybe with a few bites of a preferred food. How you approach it and the language you use is key, so pay attention to this. Be sure to use phrases such as "First three bites, then two minutes with your toy," or "As soon as you take your three bites, you can have your toy for two minutes." Repeat these phrases over and over, in response to resistance and until a bite is taken. Give a lot of praise and encourage bite number two and then three, using the same approach. Make the goal to finish all the food before he can be done but break it into "sections of bites." Make it doable and keep the reward short but often.

Try not to allow your child to get picky about textures or certain foods. If she begins to show signs of this problem, gagging, complaining, or never eating it, bring in the above recommendation as part of the eating routine. If unaddressed, the picky eater will start to develop a behavior related to eating that may involve gagging, meltdowns, or refusals. This will increase over time and will be much more difficult to

△ *Try not to allow your child to get picky about textures or certain foods. If she begins to show signs of this, gagging, complaining, never eating it, start teaching compliance as part of the eating routine.*

overcome later on, especially if there are underlying sensory or behavioral issues.

Heart Struggles

As a parent, especially a first-time parent, hearing any kind of bad news about your child is less than ideal news and never something you expect or want to experience. We've had quite a lot of unfavorable news about our children. I call it news because looking back, it wasn't necessarily bad news, but it was news that had the potential to be life-changing.

As new parents, we were devastated the first time we received news that our first born had a heart murmur. At one week old, Ryanne had gained almost a pound above her birth weight, at two weeks we were anxious to see how much more she had gained. She was happy, and she was eating really well, and we felt good about her progress. When the doctor listened to her heart, she listened for a long time and finally said to us that she had a heart murmur. Neither one of us really understood what that meant but hearing news about her heart led us to assume the worst. We left the doctor's office not sure about anything but knowing that she had something wrong with her heart, and we were devastated.

We took a slight detour home, crying the entire time. We were both so sad we couldn't speak to each other. Had we known that what she had was a very common heart murmur often found in infants, with a great chance of healing on its own, we would have handled the news a lot better. To our detriment, we did not ask our doctor a lot of questions about the murmur. Because of this, we worried unnecessarily. If you are faced with news you don't understand, ask questions. We learned this lesson the hard way but were much better prepared when we were told our two sons had heart murmurs, more specifically Atrial Septal Defects (ASD), and that these murmurs would not close on their own. They would both need to be surgically repaired.

When we first learned that Jack and Jesse had heart defects, we were upset but hopeful they would repair on their own. When we were told they would both need a procedure or surgery to repair the defect, we were, again, hoping it would be the much less invasive procedure. When the heart procedure for Jack turned into open-heart surgery, we were devastated.

We drove to UC Davis for Jack's procedure, expecting a small incision in his groin, a one-night stay in the hospital, and a quick recovery. Soon after the start of the procedure, the surgeon came out and told us they were unable to do the heart procedure. He told us that the hole in his heart was too big and our son would need open-heart surgery. I was writing in this book when we got this news. Not the worst news possible, but obviously not something we were prepared to hear. I cried a little, then stopped, then cried a little more. *My son needed heart surgery?* We knew this was a risk going into the original procedure, but of course we never expected it. Instead, we started preparing for more happy juice, a much larger IV, and a scar on his chest that would stay forever.

No one can ever tell you why your family must go through extra, beyond the normal realm of parenting. It's a part of life. In no way does this make it easier to deal with, but it does encourage you to suck it up and get through it. It was a difficult task indeed, but what helped us through it was to think about the children and their families that were living with something much bigger and scarier. Jack's issue could be fixed, and pretty easily, aside from the open-heart part. Some families have to accept that there is no fix and nothing can be done.

Several years ago, our family attended a birthday party at a miracle ranch in Northern California. This place was created for a little boy with a severe heart condition, requiring him to have seven heart surgeries by the time he was ten years old. He was not expected to live past the age of twelve. This "Miracle Ranch" was built by the boy's dad as a place for his son to grow up and help him forget about his reality. After a few years, it became a place for other children with a terminal illness to go as an escape from their real-life medical procedures and routines. Now, I can accept heart surgery and deal with it, but knowing my child was going to die, during childhood, I cannot imagine. I really try not to think about it. You may be a parent who has experienced this tragedy, and

△ *Jack's issue could be fixed, and pretty easily, aside from the open-heart part. Some families have to accept that there is no fix, and nothing can be done.*

my heart goes out to you. You would probably tell us that you went through it one day at a time finding grace for the moment. Bless you for your strength and courage to keep going.

After the first failed attempt at closing his ASD, Jack needed a few hours to sleep off the anesthesia. He woke up irritated and confused, but overall his first trip to the hospital was pleasant and left him with thoughts of happiness and popsicles. His next experience would be different. Maybe it would start worry free, but I was certain he would not leave as happy, and he wouldn't want to come back. Fortunately, he forgot, quickly, and his pain went away. Of course, the scar will remind us every day of what we went through, but he won't remember or care about the details. In fact, he is very proud of his scar and loves that he shares one with his brother. We, on the other hand, worried, planned, missed work, worried more, and then accepted it, knowing we would re-live it forever. But for us, it was one big medical event that fixed the problem, and I feel blessed that this is all we have had to go through so far, beyond the normal realms of parenting of course.

Leading up to Jack's surgery was crazy and stressful. We had several illnesses circulating our home before the surgery. His older sister and I had strep throat two weeks before the surgery date, but I did not want to reschedule, yet all the while, I worried that he would have an infection in his body during the surgery. He stayed healthy and never showed symptoms of strep.

The days leading up to it got more difficult. Human nature forces us to think of the negative side of everything. If there is less than one percent chance of a complication, I imagined it happening. Although I never felt nervous, every night before bed, my mind would visualize Jack on a bed having his chest cut open and his sternum sawed in half. This, of course, kept me awake and I didn't sleep well for several nights leading up to the surgery.

The day of and morning before the surgery is difficult to remember. I felt blah, blank, and weak. I was weak from a lack of sleep and weak from the exhaustion of stress. I was out of sorts from the surrealism of it all. Even as I sat in the waiting room, praying, writing, texting, it still felt as if it were someone else's child. A quick periodic update from the nurse brought me back to reality, but I kept waiting for her to come back with bad news, and waiting for the horrible feeling that would come with it. The confusion of sorting out and deciphering the heavy heart I felt would not register with my brain. I don't remember how long it took, but finally, one of Jack's surgeon's nurses came out to talk with us. She told us everything went well, the hole had been stitched up, and they were getting ready to wheel him to his room. It was over! The fear and emotions we had been carrying for the last few weeks left with a huge sigh and tears of relief.

The next few days in the hospital were pretty rough. Jack was up and down with pain and agitation. It took him several hours to sleep off the anesthesia, and it was a long process. I slept less than three hours, jumping up every ten to twenty minutes every time Jack woke up, screaming in pain or from confusion. The morphine they were giving him caused him to have short periods of screaming as if he were possessed. He became afraid of pain caused by anything, from taking his blood pressure to pulling tape from his skin. His catheter was uncomfortable, and after they took it out it made urination painful.

Nurses were coming in every twenty minutes to draw blood, give meds, change fluids, do chest x-rays, drain catheter bags, and check vitals. The beeping that went on every ten minutes telling them to change fluids or readjust a wire made it impossible for us to relax or sleep the first few days. A few days was all he needed and Jack was out of the hospital after just fifty hours. The first day was horrible, but we all adjusted, and Jack got to go home sooner than most kids after having open-heart surgery.

We were so relieved to have that part of our lives over. We were ready for the adjustments necessary for his recovery and knew that we would be reliving this experience again when it was Jesse's turn.

Thankfully, Jesse's surgery went extremely well. It was very similar to Jack's, and it being our second time going through it we were mentally and emotionally tougher. Jesse seemed to have a much easier time with recovery than Jack. He wasn't in as much pain, and he didn't need to take his pain medication once we left the hospital. After going home, he never once complained of pain in his chest, which is something I remember vividly from Jack's recovery. Jesse seems to have a higher tolerance for pain, which may be why his recovery seemed to go more smoothly.

Less Common But Strange Issues: Nursemaid's Elbow

This is not a stage or a milestone but a good piece of information to know. After five kids, we had our first experience with "nurse maids elbow," which is basically a fancy name for a slight dislocation of the elbow. We had just gotten a new jump house, with a few slides going in to a ball pit area. I was inside the house and the boys were jumping. Joe was twenty months. I heard Joe start crying, and when he didn't stop after a few minutes, I went out to check. He was in the bottom area holding his wrist and forearm, crying and saying "ouch." I brought him inside and tried to entice him to reach and grab for something, like his blanket or his milk. He reached with his left hand a little but would not move his right. He kept saying "ouch" and holding his arm. I thought for sure it was broken.

I took him to the emergency room and waited. Joe never moved his right arm! We went in to a small room, and the triage doctor came in asking questions. "Did you pick him up by his hands, wrists, forearms?" Of course, I was thinking, "No way!" It sounded like he was fishing for details that would imply child abuse. I got a little on the defensive and explained that he was holding his arm so I picked him up in a cradle position. I scooped him. After a few more questions he told me that the way Joe was holding his arm was typical of "nurse maids elbow," which I had not heard before. Apparently it was a very common injury. Not knowing what the heck it was, I really thought Joe's arm was broken. The doctor said he would have to twist his arm and bend his hand to his shoulder to have it pop back in place and said that if this was the problem, Joe would be using his arm normally within a few minutes. After the twist and pop back in to place, Joe quickly became the energetic, talkative little guy and was swinging his arm and pointing at things within a minute. I thought it very interesting to have been clueless about such a common thing when I have five kids and have never experienced it.

Vision Problems

Plugged tear ducts are not uncommon and happen more often than we know about. It can be rough for both you and Baby. It will look a lot like goopy eyes that never clear. They may be crusty and glossed over with a filmy substance covering the eyes. Jesse had this issue, and for him it required a very uncomfortable procedure that involved suctioning the "gunk" from his tear ducts with a tiny suction tube. This was not a fun procedure, but it was necessary.

Other less common vision issues can be a misalignment of the eyes. Otherwise known as "lazy eye," the incidence of a wandering eye can cause drastic problems later in life. It can become an issue of one eye "turning off" from the lack of connection to the brain, which may result in the eye becoming permanently blind. If you notice any alignment issues, get your baby or child to the pediatrician and then hopefully to a specialist, as soon as possible.

Misshapen Head and Helmet Wearing

It is not uncommon for an infant's head to develop a flat spot or odd shape. This really depends on a number of factors. It may be related to an extra sleepy baby that prefers to favor one side of the head while sleeping. Often, and more common, is a flat spot that can develop at the back of the head. This is generally caused from babies spending a lot of time on their backs.

Jesse's head was developing an odd shape for a few reasons. One was that he was very sleepy and he didn't move a lot when he slept. He also preferred to sleep on one side of his head, which was related to having tight neck muscles that pulled his head to one side more than the other. We started noticing after a few months that it was not only flat in the back, but that he was also developing a flat spot on the left side of his head.

Treatment for misshapen heads is constantly changing. The best way for parents to do this is to give their babies more tummy time and adjust their head position while they sleep. This will influence positive results for babies growing normally and with no underlying issues. With Jesse and his hypotonia (weak muscles throughout his body), tummy time did not work because he was too weak to keep his head up or turn it from side to side. He also didn't sit up until he was almost a year, which made it difficult to keep the pressure off his flat spots.

At nine months, Jesse was fitted for a cranial molding helmet. He wore this for ten hours a day with mini breaks for cooling and relief from the pressure. He wore the helmet for four months through the summer, in 100 plus degree weather. It was really difficult, but it did help. His head will always have a unique shape, but I believe the cranial molding helmet reduced the severity of his flat spots.

It's never easy to accept that your child may struggle in life, or that a possibility exists for surgery, medical procedures, daily medication for life, or worse. It seems that illness and health struggles are becoming much more common issues for families. Parenting is already difficult and scary enough without adding more worry to it. Please know that as a parent, you are much stronger than you believe yourself to be, and if a challenge presents itself, no matter what the issue, you will have the strength and ability to rise to the occasion.

△ *Please know that as a parent, you are much stronger than you believe yourself to be, and if a challenge presents itself, no matter what the issue, you will have the strength and ability to rise to the occasion.*

△ Notes

Eleven

The Minivan

What's in a minivan? Why is it loved by some and hated by so many others? Is it the "soccer mom" stigma that attracts the soccer-mom-to-be and repulses the hip, stylish, latest in everything mom? Could it be that someone who drives a minivan is or might be considered uncool? I've always wondered why so many are sickened by the thought of owning this wonderfully liberating vehicle. It's not just an uneasy feeling, but they become enraged at the thought and suggestion that they would actually drive such a car. I'm sure no one ever dreams about owning their own minivan. My dream car was, for the longest time, an Acura, and not just any Acura. I dreamt of a white, four-door Acura Integra, with a sunroof and spoiler.

I first fell in love with this car on a high school volleyball trip. Our bus had stopped at a McDonald's just off Interstate 5 in Williams, California, and there she was, parked outside the McDonalds, glistening in the sunlight. Although I saw her for only about fifteen minutes, I had found my car. I thought about that Acura for many years and obviously still have some feelings about owning such a cute, sporty, cool car. I was in high school, however, and of course, reality changed as I got older and realized it would be years before I had a nice car. Needless to say, it never worked out with the Acura, and I

△ *Like so many, I never wanted to drive a minivan. No way would I have been caught dead in one. I was a young, cool mom with style, and of course, an image to uphold. What would a minivan do to my image?*

moved on to something else, which was pretty much anything my parents could afford.

From a single college girl to a student teacher and mom of two, I had been the proud owner of a Plymouth, a Volvo, a Toyota Tercel, and a 1990 Nissan Pathfinder (not at the same time of course). I loved all of these because they were mine and fun to drive. After becoming a mother, I wanted an SUV more than anything, and I got one! I really loved my Pathfinder. It was cool, comfortable, and it had a lot of room for our kids. Yes, it was a little on the pricey side, and it got terrible gas mileage, but I didn't care about any of that practical stuff because it was an SUV and not a minivan. Like so many, I *never* wanted to drive a minivan. No way would I have been caught dead in one. I was a young, cool mom, with style, and of course, an image to uphold. What would a minivan do to my image? Boy, was I naive and shallow! Not that SUV owners are naive and shallow. I only say this because I know now what I was missing and was lucky enough to have realized it. I can look back at it and I am thankful I had a change of heart.

> "We had an Expedition when our girls were born. It was huge and difficult for me to get the girls in and out. We rented a minivan for an out of town trip and realized how convenient and spacious it was. I never, ever wanted to drive a minivan, but when we got back from our trip we bought one. I wouldn't drive anything else."
>
> — Rebecca, veteran mother of 3

I was able to test drive my mom's van when our kids were little, and I realized right away how much better, more practical, roomier, and more convenient a minivan was. Very few moms have the chance to test a minivan for weeks at a time, but I know if they did, they'd fall in love just like I did. Like most things, the minivan only gets better with experience! They've actually been given a cute body style and are getting better and more practical with each new year in production.

What is so sad about this is that so many mothers (and dads, too) will never have the chance or want the chance to test a minivan. Unfortunately, the idea of driving one is so ridiculous to so many parents; many will never know what they are missing. I realize how hard it is to get over that negative stigma that comes with being a minivan owner. My sister is an example of a minivan hater. She never liked the idea of a minivan, and like me, she was never going to drive one. She didn't even want to hear why I thought they were so much better. When she had her first child, she of course bought a larger vehicle. Any guesses on what it was? Yep! It was an SUV. And it was a very nice SUV. It was cute, roomy, and of course, it was new. I tried to talk her out of it and fought hard for all us minivan groupies. Her stubbornness and her image powered through. She likes her SUV, but I really believe she would love a minivan!

Now, us minivan owners and aspiring minivan owners have a lot of passion and powerful persuasion techniques that should work for changing minds. In reality, unless someone experiences the perks and benefits on their own or gives up their fight to maintain a certain image, it is difficult to persuade an SUV lover to cross over. I was an SUV lover through and through, and although my mom tried to tell me that a minivan was so much better, I always replied with a "yeah, but..." I couldn't justify "yeah, butting" my way through the actual experience of using her minivan. After driving with her for a few weeks, I was hooked. I know how hard it is to persuade, because I could not be persuaded with success stories. I had to find out on my own. Although my passion and persuasion might get your attention, it's likely you won't become a minivan owner without a direct "ah ha" revelation, but here it goes anyway.

I've talked a lot about how awesome minivans are, but I haven't given much evidence to support my claim. Here are just a few reasons why I love my minivan.

If you have not already experienced how difficult it can be to get an infant car seat into or out of a car, you're in for it! Imagine running to a store, any store with your baby. You park the car, shop for awhile and you come out to find someone parked very close to you. So close in fact, you can hardly squeeze your new, larger-sized baby figure between them. You squeeze yourself between your car and theirs, open the door (only part way because the other car is so close), and try to fit your baby and the infant seat into the car, only to realize the seat won't fit. You can't open the door wide enough to get your baby in the car. I've had this happen several times, and it is so frustrating, especially if you're a brand-new mom and your hormones are running your life!

The first time this happened, I cried. Yes, I know, it's a silly thing to cry about, but as I mentioned previously sometimes you don't have much control. I had to walk to the other side, hoping I had more room, open the door, climb in the car, and set the infant seat into its base. This was not easy.

Think of the same scenario, but instead of *trying* to open the door and crawling in on the other side, the sliding door automatically slides open, leaving you with the space and clearance you need. There's no climbing inside to put the car seat in (as I found with SUVs and large trucks), and you aren't breaking your back leaning down, which was the case when we had a sedan. And who can argue with the automatic sliding doors? Automatic sliding doors are not something you really need all the time but can be so nice to have when it's raining or dark. One little push of a button and your door is open for you when you arrive. It's almost like having a chauffeur!

Minivans are considered safer than SUVs because they don't have as much of a risk for rolling in an accident, although all cars get better and safer with each new production year. However, vans are lower to the ground, and have a wider body, which allows for better and safer weight distribution. Our first was a 2006 Honda Odyssey, which I absolutely loved! It was on the higher end of the price scale, but we wanted to pay more for the added safety features in the Honda design. As with many "EX" editions, our van had front and rear sensors that sounded and beeped faster as you approached foreign objects, or as they approached you, such as pedestrians or shopping carts. It also had a camera in the rear that allowed us to see directly behind us as we were backing out. In all our years with our minivans we've had zero bike fatalities. We haven't hit anything else either. After our first Honda Odyssey, we upgraded

△ *We've never had to sacrifice wardrobes for fitting the family. With a minivan, we can do both!*

to driving a 2011 Honda Odyssey. It seated eight, and had the more attractive body style. We are still driving this van and it has been as wonderful as our first, and it won't be the last van we drive.

> "I switched to a minivan because I was jealous of the other minivan moms that could just press a button and tell their kids to get out and not worry about them closing the door."
> — Stephanie, mother of 3

Another great feature of newer vans is the option to roll down the back windows. Although they don't roll down completely, it is nice that we can give our kids some fresh air. The back seats fold into the floor to make the back as big as a small truck bed, so it's similar to a small truck, but with more functionality. Many would argue that a van is not nearly as cool as a truck (my husband included,) but when it comes to functionality, it's got a truck beat by a landslide. Also, the van is always covered so wet weather is never a problem. We once purchased a "power wheels" John Deere Jeep for our kids, and we were able to fit it in the back of the van, with enough room for two adults in the front seats and two kids in the back. I was pretty impressed with this and fell in love with my van all over again! When all seats are up, our van can fit eight people including their bags. We've never had to sacrifice wardrobes for fitting the family. We can do both! I'll admit, when you have a family of six, seven, and especially eight, and are packing suitcases, baby gear, art supplies, and movies, etc, it does get a little cramped. But if you pack it right, it works.

△ *Owning a minivan may never be a dream for most parents. Hopefully it will at minimum, be a realistic option that they are willing to pursue, someday.*

Some vans have bench seats in the middle row, as well as in the third row. These bench seats don't always have the fold down option, but can be better for older kids and often allow one more person for a total of eight. We have bucket seats in the front, bucket and bench-like seats in the middle that can be removed, and a bench seat in the very back. The bench seat can fold down for seating two, with less space for stuff, or it can fold down to seat one, for a little more space. It's really nice to have this option. We've had a minivan for years, and still have yet to discover all of the wonderful things about them.

In comparing other vehicles to the family minivans, SUVs and large trucks specifically, the body styles of the SUVs and trucks win, hands down. However, body styles of the minivan are getting more attractive and almost "cool" and the benefits of the minivan, as a family car are so much more, when comparing them to the other family car choices. The functionality of a minivan as well as the space, safety, price, and even gas mileage, can't be matched! Owning a minivan may never be a dream for most parents. Hopefully, it will at minimum be a realistic option that they are willing to pursue, someday.

> **"The thought of a minivan made me feel like I was giving up youth and my cool. I went from a car to an SUV to purposely skip over the minivan. Then I saw my friends who had kids, and all the room and flexibility they had with their vans. Now in a van I'm so happy! I may drive a minivan after the kids move out—it's just so nice!"**
>
> — Chrystina, mother of 3

I realize for some, minivans just aren't in their deck of cards. Some live in big cities, where parking is tough and space is limited. A minivan just wouldn't be practical for a family in the city, especially if the family doesn't drive often. Also, for people with only a few kids, the benefits of the minivan wouldn't be as substantial, and the comparison between the van and the SUV would seem pointless.

My why for writing this book was to give new and unseasoned moms, and dads too, some practical and useful information. I believe the minivan deserves a shout out as well. It is advice and a recommendation that I believe will only make parenting and carting children easier. I spend at least three hours a day in the car. Two of which involve several pick-ups, drop offs, loading and unloading of a lot of stuff and kids. As they get older and more involved in their athletic activities, the comfort, accommodations, and space of the minivan is becoming crucial for an overall positive shuttle service experience, for all of us. Keep your mind open to the possibilities and you too may experience the incredible benefits of owning your very own minivan.

△ Notes

Twelve

Just My Opinion

I've learned many things about what to have and not to have
in a home when kids are around. When it's other people's
kids, you can move or remove things to prevent damage, both
to the kids and to your valuables. When it's someone else's
kids you can put your things back when they leave, but when
it's your own, it's a lot more of a pain to have a house that
constantly needs rearranging. And trust me, if your kid is curious, he will touch, pick up, and knock over anything that can
be touched, picked up, and knocked over. All kids are curious.

What to Have

A mess is just unavoidable and to be expected, so just have it!
If you try to keep it neat all the time, you will have very little
time to enjoy your kids. I tried for several years to keep my
house neat, but as the kids kept coming, the mess became
more difficult to control. Every day, I would pick up, and pick
up, and pick up again. Sometimes I'd gather up the same toy
three times in one day! This was a daily after work activity.
Finally, I realized that I needed to accept the mess. I have
never accepted it fully, but I have allowed myself to be ok
with a less-than-spotless home. I also realized that limiting the
clutter, and the amount of toys available to play with helped
limit the mess.

What to have:

△ A messy house!

△ Batteries of all sizes and shapes.

△ Small screwdrivers for use indoors on toys and other household items.

△ Scissors in the kitchen or other areas of the house that are easily accessible.

△ A plan for organizing important documents, schedules, etc.

△ A Swiss Army knife or multi-tool for home and travel.

△ Flashlights, large and small.

△ A baby book for each of your kids that you ACTUALLY write in.

△ Sugar (in moderation).

Now, messy and dirty are completely different. A dirty home can be unsanitary and can teach your kids the wrong idea about living. My advice is to dust, sweep, and mop once in awhile, to clean up spills as soon as you notice them, keep coloring and writing utensils out of reach, and NEVER allow your kids to eat anywhere but where food belongs. If they eat anywhere but the table, you will no doubt find food all over the house. We addressed this rule very early and it has worked so far. However, sometimes the older kids still "forget" that food is to remain in the kitchen or dining area. At thirteen years old, Ryanne thinks the rules don't apply to her.

> **"A good mom has dirty floors, a sticky oven, and happy kids!"**
>
> — Katie S, new mother of 1

Batteries are a necessity. I always keep batteries of all sizes on hand just in case. I can't count the number of times this strategy has come in handy. Whether it's a new birthday present received or given that requires batteries, the TV remote suddenly dying, or the baby's favorite musical toy stops working, having the right batteries to solve these problems can save a fight or meltdown.

As important as stocking up on batteries is, having the right screwdrivers to get to those dead batteries is equally necessary. A handy set of mini screwdrivers with different shapes and sizes is also a must have in our house. We have used these small tools mostly on opening and fixing kids' toys, but we've had several successful attempts at unlocking bathroom doors with mini flat head screwdrivers.

Don't forget to have the scissors in a convenient location, like the kitchen, but out of reach of little hands. This very useful tool will get plenty of deserved attention and recognition. You never know when you'll encounter that "tough as nails" cereal bag that just won't cooperate or tags that won't break. Having the right tool when you need it really can be priceless.

The Swiss Army knife or other similar multi-tool can be a life-saver, and it is an item that my grandpa insisted his children and adult grandchildren always had available. I can think of many moments, at home and on the road, where small scissors, a mini pocket knife, or tiny screw driver saved a situation. Make sure to have a tool that works for you, but is also difficult for a child to figure out. And don't forget the flashlights for home and travel! These, too, will always be needed.

Having a plan for organizing your life isn't essential if you like searching for hours for that birth certificate you know you have. Locating and storing important documents and saving and protecting our kids' best work is a daily task in our life. Establishing a place for everything, before you need it, has also been very helpful. Spending the least amount of time possible on filing and organizing paperwork is important, *and this will only work if everything has a place.*

Similar to this concept is the storing and organizing of pictures, which can be very time-consuming without a ready-made system. A system for printing and updating photo albums can save a tremendous amount of time. Having the albums to put them in is also handy. You won't realize this necessity until after you've taken hundreds, if not thousands of pictures with your digital camera. If you are tech savvy or a media mogul, you may not see a need for organizing your pictures into albums. Pictures typically either stay on the camera or remain digital images that have been uploaded to your computer or taken on a phone. All of these photos become difficult to sort through and share, however, when your iPhoto or phone grows to thousands of images. If you want to have some of your pictures in the form of a traditional, hard copy photo, I recommend printing a few of your best pictures every three to four months.

Have a baby book for each of your kids. Do, do, do it for all of them! You may want to compare milestones for each child or write in the cute things they say. They will love to see it when they have kids of their own and the milestones are more relevant to them. It's so cool to read about yourself as a kid, look at your old drawings, stories, and other moments, and to share them with your own kids. My mom kept a record of milestones in my baby book, although not as thorough as my sister's, because I was the *second* child. I loved looking through my moments and comparing it with my own kids'. I didn't keep a good record of any of my kids. Joe, the fifth child, didn't get anything! I don't know that we even have any pictures of him as a baby and if we do there aren't many. We do, however, have this book, which provides us with more stories than any baby book could. Whatever record you decide to keep, keep it handy and write often. I wish I had done it more and had started sooner.

Sugar is an unavoidable battle you will face often with your kids. When they are little, it is easy to prevent them from eating it, and even knowing about it's existence. They figure out quickly, however, that they are missing out. Avoiding it and preventing them from having ANY sugar can backfire. When they have more freedom, their curiosity will prompt them to sneak and overindulge in sweets, when they can. They may even steal a bag of marshmallows, lock you out of the house, and hide in the closet eating the entire bag!

Personality and example play a huge part in a child's desire to eat and indulge in sweets. We've allowed a little sugar consistently over the years, and we have a few that can tolerate some and only need small amounts. We have one child that can and does tolerate a lot. It comes back to teaching and modeling good choices and behaviors. If they understand that they have the control to make decisions, you can usually guide them into making the right choices about sweets, as opposed to dictating to them what choices they WILL make.

What NOT to have in a house full of kids

△ A coffee table.

△ A low TV stand.

△ Low-standing house plants.

△ A lot of stuff (clothing included).

△ Porcelain tea set (or anything porcelain for kids).

△ Toxic chemicals within reach of little hands.

Don't have a coffee table—unless you want your kid to get a fat lip or stitches, or just a really bad goose egg on her forehead. None of these are fun, and kids will no doubt get them somewhere else. Don't add to their risk of injury by having a sharp-edged target for them to hit. When toddlers are learning to walk and are unsteady with their hands and feet, they often fall, slip, or lose their grasp. And because they often learn to walk by holding on to things, anything sharp is dangerous. When they are older and are steady on their feet, they start climbing, jumping, wrestling, and it's often on or around the couch and coffee table. They will fall, and if a coffee table exists, they will hit it! My suggestion is a soft-edged ottoman. It can work like a coffee table or a footrest, but it won't break the skin on impact. It also gives them another base for jumping. We still haven't had either, and it's nice to give the kids more room to play, but I will be getting an ottoman, if only to rest my feet when I sit down.

A low TV stand is another undesirable piece of furniture, unless you don't mind crayons in the DVD player or handprints and food on the TV. A wall mounted TV is much more common now than when my kids were little, and it's definitely safer. Other electronics must also be kept out of reach in order to prolong the life of your "toys" and also your voice. It gets old repeatedly telling your toddler, "don't touch" while he looks at you with the evil eye, and then touches what he's not supposed to touch. It can also be frustrating when you realize your Nintendo Wii (or other gaming device) has become the new piggy bank and can no longer be used for entertainment. Avoid the confrontation and make your entertainment area kid and baby friendly.

△ **TIP:** *Go small with stuff early in their lives, and you will limit the disappointment they experience, or at least the disappointment you can control.*

Houseplants are a bad idea if you have curious crawlers or walkers that don't know the difference between dirt and crackers. Be prepared for a dead plant and an extremely dirty floor. Having a plant above the reach of little fingers might work, if you can keep it alive. But if you're like me, you can't.

If you have a lot of stuff, it can run your life! Go easy on the stuff. The more "stuff" kids have (clothes, shoes, toys) the more cleaning and laundry you will be doing. My kids really struggled with keeping clothes in their drawers, and separating the clean clothes from the dirty ones. Clean or dirty, they ALL seemed to make it into the hamper. As if I didn't already have enough laundry to wash. I don't know how many batches of clean laundry I used to do, but I did too many. I finally realized they had too much! I downsized a little of everything and noticed a lot of a difference. So, I downsized more, and was doing a lot less. The kids had less to do as well. What I found was that they all had their favorite toys and their favorite clothes, and they didn't notice when something not as cherished was removed.

It's not easy to de-clutter and de-stress your house. It feels a little like you are throwing money in the trash. Remember that you are making your life and your kids' lives easier by getting rid of stuff. You can recycle your goods at your local Goodwill or Salvation Army store, and your kids will learn about giving. This may even motivate them to give away more, if they help you with the cleanout. Sometimes, it helps to focus on what to keep instead of what to donate. If it's not an item that creates excitement for you or them, it may not be worth keeping. Also, remember that if you don't overdo it in the beginning, you'll avoid the torture of cleaning house later, and the waste of money from unnecessary purchases. Limiting what they have MUST happen early. If you go big at holidays and birthdays, your kids will always expect big or bigger. Go small with stuff early in their lives, and you will limit the disappointment they experience, or at least the disappointment you can control.

Porcelain toys can be cute and exciting, for both the child and parent (mostly mom), but they are nothing but trouble. When our girls were three and eighteen months, Santa (grandma and grandpa), brought a cute, porcelain tea set for them to use during their tea parties. This did not work out well, as we found out a few months later how Reese really felt about tea parties.

Ryanne and Reese were in their room having tea at three years and eighteen months old. I was on the phone in the kitchen with a colleague, venting about something. I was distracted, of course, but not so distracted that I didn't notice Reese running toward the kitchen with a blue and white polka dotted, porcelain tea cup in her hand. Before I could stop her, she threw the cup towards me and onto the tile floor. It shattered! I moaned, told her "no," and started sweeping up the mess, but I continued the discussion with my colleague. As I poured the last few pieces of porcelain from the dust pan into the trash, I heard little footsteps running toward me. I looked over just in time to see Reese throw another cute, polka dotted porcelain tea cup onto the tile floor. It, too, shattered!

Two years later, we found out that our little three-year-old Reese was a budding athlete as she threw her porcelain doll onto the floor at Grammy and Papa's, and it shattered! She loved to throw things, as most kids do, which is why it is best to avoid shattered toys by saving porcelain toys for big kids. Looking back, it makes sense now why she enjoys playing sports as much as she does.

Preparing For a Sibling

A child who is confident and comfortable without mom or dad's attention will adjust well to a brother or sister. If having more than one child is part of the family plan, help your first-born prepare for a sibling early by teaching them independence. If they are comfortable playing by themselves and can hold it together when mom and dad aren't around, the need to keep all the attention on themselves won't be as strong. All of our kids were excited, loving, and very sweet to their new siblings. They never acted jealous or acted out. There was never aggression or irritation toward the baby or us. I truly believe that an independent child can adjust more easily to any new moment or change in their environment, but it does require early preparation.

Tummy or Back

Everyone feels different about this very controversial and scary topic, but ultimately it's up to the parent. My mom always said, "I don't know how any of my kids survived" because when we were babies, we all slept on our tummies. But, we survived, and most babies will benefit from tummy time, and an early introduction to it. Mine did.

Early introduction to tummy time can happen as early as a few days after birth. It may give peace of mind if you stay within arms reach during the first few weeks of practice. If you are close by, it really doesn't matter if they are awake or sleeping. Awake time spent on their tummies will strengthen their neck and back muscles, and acclimate them to the position. As time goes on, they will get more and more comfortable being face down, and the time spent distracting them will begin to look and feel more like play. To explain a bit further, it was always helpful when I distracted my babies during their tummy experiences. My face, a toy, or something exciting to look at helped to extend happy time by a few seconds, and then minutes as they became more comfortable. My babies protested tummy practice for the first several weeks, but I encouraged them and insisted that they give it time. If it makes you nervous, stick around until you become more comfortable with the position.

Tummy time while Baby sleeps is a little scarier because he is sleeping, and you aren't always nearby to watch and check on him. After a lot of practice on his tummy, you will notice that his neck and back gets stronger, and he is able to lift his head and turn from side to side. If he can accomplish this, you should feel more confident in laying him down on his tummy. Babies really do sleep better in this position.

I felt very comfortable putting my babies on their tummy at naptime, if I was nearby to check. As they got stronger, I noticed that they were able to move their heads easily, and I felt much better about leaving them alone, although they were still sleeping and napping in a bassinet that I could move when I needed to leave the room. This made it easy to keep them close. Soon, after they moved to a crib, they were rolling over a little. It's an exciting day when you put your baby down on his back for a nap in his crib, and when you go in to get him,

△ *It's an exciting day when you put your baby down on his back for a nap and you go in to get him and he is on his stomach.*

he is on his stomach. When it happens and he rolls from his back to his tummy, it can be scary, especially for a new mom. In my experience, once my babies rolled to their tummies, the tummy or back dilemma was no longer an issue. If they were strong enough to get themselves to their tummies, they were strong enough to roll themselves back. It's hard not to worry when they first start rolling back to front, especially at night. When they start to do this often, be happy they have graduated to this next level.

Germs Are Okay

In my opinion, and my mother's, and my mother's mother, germs are okay. Research shows that exposure to germs, dirt, dust, pets, or most other things we try to avoid, can reduce a child's risk for having sensitivities to illness, pets, dust, allergies, and other things. I'm not going to get into the science of it all, because frankly, I don't know it, but I truly believe that some allergies and sensitivities are very much related to genetics. However, early exposure to "sick germs," as we call them in our house, means less trouble with them later. A baby that experiences very few illnesses or exposure to illness when young will likely get sick more often when he is mixed with other school aged kids and a lot of sick germs. A kid that goes to daycare and gets sick every other week in the first two or three years, will rarely get sick once he has started elementary school, when germs are much more rampant.

My children were exposed to a lot of dirt, dust, pet dander, germs, and who knows what else when they were young. Binkies on the floor, blankets with dog hair, a dusty table you could write your name on. I could go on. It wasn't as bad as it sounds, but the point is that germs are unavoidable and not always a bad thing. I was exposed to the same "conditions," as were my siblings, and we are all very healthy and allergy free, with very few, if any sensitivities. As my mom did before me, and her mom before her, I have not focused on avoiding germs or anything else that might be considered "less than clean." My kids have have been exposed to all of it. To this day, not one of them, has had any issues with allergens from inside our home. They are extremely healthy. They did get sick from the sick germs early in their lives, and often, but once in kindergarten and the early grades when the germs hit, it rarely knocked them down. The number of school days they missed due to illness were minimal and continue to be. They rarely miss school and learning opportunities, and I don't miss work. Like everything else in this book, your response to this is ultimately up to you, but I've included it as something else to ponder.

Additionally, hand washing limits the exposure to germs and bacteria, while also preventing the body from creating antibodies to better protect itself from these very important immune strengthening organisms. Like I mentioned earlier, I am staying out of the science, but I encourage you to do research on this topic. Understanding more on this will reassure you when your kid forgets to wash his hands before eating. I rarely wash my hands (yes, there are exceptions), and I seldom emphasize this with my kids, although there are exceptions to this as well.

When to Introduce a Sippy Cup

The exact time for trying out a sippy cup really depends on the child. Some babies become very attached to their bottles, and sippy cups are much more difficult for them to accept. However, timing is important and waiting too long to offer and introduce a sippy cup can make it near impossible to convince your little one to try it. In my experience and expertise, I've realized it's best to wait until they are really comfortable with drinking from a bottle, and even somewhat familiar with eating solids of different textures.

Snack time with finger foods is a great time to offer a different drinking cup. This way he isn't pressured to drink but can if he chooses. The food will likely make him thirsty, and he will want to drink, or at least try it. It is important to stay firm once you introduce the sippy cup at snack. If he gets upset and throws a fit, DO NOT give him the bottle. Simply offer the sippy cup and let him choose to drink from it or not. If he chooses not to, he will remain thirsty. Eventually, his thirst and need to check it out will persuade him to start trying it until it becomes routine.

It really depends on the child's personality, but typically, he won't really like, want or accept a sippy cup until around twelve to fifteen months. Avoid replacing the morning and evening bottles until he will drink most beverages from the sippy, including milk. When he seems ready to move on to replacing his morning or evening bottle with a sippy cup, start with replacing one at a time. It can be tough for some babies to let go of what is so comforting, but again, if you wait too long, the habit will be much more difficult to break.

Reacting to a Fall

The way you react to a fall, hard or soft, is how your child will react. If you gasp and come running, the worried look on your face will scare your baby, and she will likely cry. However, if you stay put, give an *uh oh*, and keep calm, you can teach toughness, and usually ward off crying. Even a hard fall can be brushed off if the child has learned to do this from a very early age. Now, if it is a hard knock on the head, crying is generally unavoidable. The fear in the child will be less if you control your reaction, and the crying will be shorter. Empathy for and acknowledgment of the injury is still important so he feels nurtured and protected. Reacting calmly and quickly and redirecting his attention to something else, will help him forget and feel better.

When Joe was still a climber, he climbed into a laundry basket before he could walk. He managed to climb over the edge, and then slid down to the inside. When he tried to climb out, the empty, very light basket tipped over. He was holding onto the top side of the basket, and as it tipped, he did a straight face plant into the carpet. He sat up, mouth pouting and eyes welling with tears. He looked at me almost like waiting for my cue on how to react but wanting to cry. I looked at him, smiled, and said "Uh oh, did you bonk?" He wiped off his worry and went straight for another go at the basket, almost unfazed by his fall.

The Binkie Fairy

Like a bottle, a binkie or pacifier is a habit that comforts your baby. This makes it really hard to take away, both for you and

Baby. Not only is it a peacemaker, but the binkie is the all controlling, all powerful cry stopping, sleep inducing, irreplaceable necessity! It's likely been a part of your family for at least a few years, and letting it go is just not possible. Yes, we've been there, several times, and we were facing this dilemma as I wrote this paragraph. Joe was almost two. He was allowed his binkie only when he slept, so it should have been easier to take it away, right? No, it wasn't, and to be honest, it's difficult anyway you look at it.

Ryanne had her binkie until just before her fourth birthday. Reese was a little over two and we were starting to notice their dependence increasing. It was also affecting Ryanne's oral development, and her front teeth were starting to push out more than they should. We decided it was time to get rid of binkies. We had no idea how to do it, and then we watched an episode of *Supernanny*. The star of this episode was the Binkie Fairy! What a great idea! We were, of course, very skeptical, but we were also without other options. We decided that the Binkie fairy would make a visit and take *all* the binkies in the house, which included both Ryanne's and Reese's. We explained to them that we were going to find all the binkies, and set them out along the windowsill for the Binkie Fairy. She, or he would come during the night, collect all the binkies, and leave behind a little gift for each of them.

Ryanne was a little older so she understood the idea enough to get excited. She ran around the house looking for binkies, for what seemed like hours, but ended up finding eight binkies—some in very strange places. If you are searching the house, be sure to look under the mattress as this is where they often end up.

We helped them line the binkies along the windowsill, and explained the trade one last time. Reese likely did not fully understand what was happening, but we hoped that she would be excited enough about her little gift that she wouldn't even remember what was missing.

Morning came and the binkies went. Left in their place, for each of the girls, was a very small little stuffed puppy. They were tiny, but they made a little noise with the gentle press of a tiny little button. They were both thrilled with their gifts. If you can believe it, they almost completely forgot about their binkies. I say almost because two days after their visit from the Binkie Fairy, Ryanne asked about her binkies and was having some withdrawals. She was a little upset, but we reminded her about her gift from the Binkie Fairy, and she went to bed with very little protest. Neither one of the girls mentioned their binkies again. Two years later we tried it with Jack. It worked again, just as it had with the girls. Definitely something to try! Although I can't guarantee its success for you, there is no harm in putting forth the effort.

Super Glue and Cuts

Using super glue for a cut that may need stitches is a safe and easy alternative to the emergency room or doctor's office. If the cut is small and not too deep, and you are contemplating taking him in for stitches, reexamine the cut. It's likely it can be closed using super glue. Looking up instructions on the internet will help you determine if it's a super glue cut, and will advise you on how to do it. The location of the cut is also an important factor in determining whether you close it with glue, or whether you have the professionals do it.

A cut on the face should be treated professionally. Most of the time, doctors and nurses know how to close a cut neatly, and the result is generally a small, clean scar. However, in our situation, Jack's cut was on his head, and we felt it could be closed using super glue. We tried it, and it worked! The process really only involves cleaning and disinfecting the cut and drying the skin on and around it. Once this is done the cut should be pushed closed and then sealed with superglue. It's important to hold the cut closed for a minute or longer to allow the glue to dry.

It took a few months for the super glue to wash off Jack's scalp, but eventually it did, and the scar is clean and small. Generally, cuts anywhere other than the face can be closed using superglue. Please remember that this is my opinion and based on my experience. I am not giving medical advice but rather offering an alternative. If the cut is large and bleeding heavily, take your child in for medical attention.

△ **FYI:** *Using super glue for a cut that may need stitches is a safe and easy alternative to the emergency room or doctor's office.*

Having a Special Needs Child

No parent wants to hear that his child is "special" and will require "special needs." However, the fact is, you can't prevent it once its there, and most of the time you can't cure it. It's a waste of energy to deny the situation and to become angry. These reactions will only create problems in an already unsettled and stressful situation. A diagnosis at the very beginning of your child's life, or even before it begins, might be more difficult to accept because you haven't had time to just be with your baby. Initial reactions tend to stem from a fear of the unknown. What does it mean? Will he live? Will it be difficult to care for him? Some conditions require more time and further investigation than others, which can also be scary.

Maybe you notice that your child isn't making eye contact or that his movements seem different than what you know to be typical. With these observations comes some investigation, leading to appointments with medical specialists, and eventually a discovery is made that your child has a genetic issue or other disability. Often times, this discovery comes without a diagnosis. The reaction will likely be sadness first, and then fear. Everyone deals with life's struggles in their own way, and the health of a child is no different. As difficult as it may be to accept, your choices are somewhat limited as to what you can choose for your child. You can love her unconditionally, listen to yourself and the doctors, understand the situation and her condition, and then finally, when you're ready, accept it. It is never easy, but it is possible.

Our special Jesse is our special gift from God. He's pure of heart, soul, and mind. He knows no different than what God has given him and to him, his life is normal. He will never feel different unless he is made to feel that way. He came to us from God, (or a higher power if this is your belief) to remind us all that we are all special in so many ways. It is also a reminder that people with special needs are people who love, laugh, learn, and share their lives completely with anyone who will let them. It is not easy caring for a child who needs extra. It takes time, money, and a lot of emotions. Jesse has had so much to overcome physically, and his physical difficulties have severely delayed his mental and emotional development. But,

△ *It is always tough to hear unfavorable news about your child, at any age. And the difficulties of raising a special needs child may always exist. But for us, and all the people in Jesse's life, we are better people because of him.*

he is happy! His happiness in life depends on his family and those that surround him.

Yes, it is always extremely tough to hear unfavorable news about your child, at any age, and the difficulties may always exist. But for us, and all the people in Jesse's life, we are better people because of him. We are more accepting of others, we understand the differences in others, and we can relate to the challenges that many confront daily. We've been through a lot with Jesse, but we see him as our angel, sent from God. It is our job to protect him and to enjoy him, and to help him to enjoy his life as much as possible.

Please remember that my intention in writing this book is not to tell you how to arrange your house or what to buy. As is anything, it's your prerogative. However, in living a busy life with my husband and five kids, we've had a lot of experience and know what only the veteran parents know. For us, these suggestions are some of the most important and helpful considerations to make. I wish someone had given me this kind of advice so I could have been prepared and ready. Instead, I learned the hard way. Perhaps my experiences were more meaningful and authentic because of it.

As for this book, our experiences and our choices for how we've lived through these experiences are just that, our choices. Because these issues reflect our choices, it ultimately boils down to our own personal opinions on how to be the best parents we can be and raise happy, healthy, confident, respectful, and loving human beings. Only time will tell if what we are doing and what we have done will accomplish this objective. But, we are off to a pretty good start so far. Now, are we prepared to raise five teenagers? Not likely, but the reality is that we will have some insight for raising teenagers *after* we've raised them. Learning on the job has its benefits, but it is reassuring to have some ideas on raising babies, toddlers and teens. If we survive the teenage years, I will most definitely be sharing our insights with you, in *Blindsided by Teenagers*.

Good Luck and welcome to motherhood!

△ Notes

Advice From Other Moms

"You can try to tell them until they are blue in the face but it will save you a lot of time if you just show them. Things that seem obvious to adults are literally nonsensical to kids. So show them how to brush their teeth by doing it yourself. Show them how to put their shoes in the bin, show them how to put their plate in the dishwasher. This sounds so silly to write, but they don't know what 'put your plate in the dishwasher' means until you show them. It took me years to learn this!"

— *Melissa, veteran mother of 6*

"Bargain with your kids when it comes to expectations. 'You can go as soon as you clean your room.' 'You can get a phone when you've kept your grades up.' 'You can have money for the movies once the laundry is folded.'"

— *Shannon, veteran mother of 2*

"Don't sweat the small things. It's so much more enjoyable if you don't. I used to never want my kids to get dirty—what fun is that!"

— *Loni, veteran mother of 4*

"When your children say to you, 'Mom, come watch me' go every time!! That time is precious, and whatever you are doing can wait."

— *Jenny, veteran mother of 2*

"Be prepared for the mom guilt of always being judged, regarding any decision. Vaccinate or not, work or stay home, cloth or disposable, breastfeed or formula...it's endless. No parent is perfect. A remedy for this is to not judge others and to give advice only when warranted. And, to be kind always, cuz most of us know what it's like to lose our $hit."

— Chrystina, mother of 3

"Try not to be freaked out about everything being so clean. Relax more and let them get dirty. Let your daughter wear whatever she wants when she is little whether it matches or not, and keep the house loud for naps."

— Tammy, veteran mom of 2

"As a grandmother I see things differently. I wish parents would have been more transparent with the younger mothers back when their kids were little, on how to deal with their toddlers' behavior the correct way."

— Elizabeth, veteran mother

"Find something early in your motherhood experience, that keeps you motivated to always move forward, with your kids, your family, your career, your purpose. One of the toughest things in parenting is the guilt that comes with missing a game, reacting unfavorably, being impatient or not having the energy to give them the attention they need and want. Working parents feel it, stay at home parents feel it. Find something that keeps you positive, that you can all do together, that moves you forward and helps others."

— Nicole, veteran mother of 5

About The Author

Nicole has been a mother since 2004. Her formal education in business and teaching does not make her an expert in motherhood. However, her experience with on the job mothering including giving birth, breastfeeding, sleep training, potty training, the terribles, and every other stage of parenting, five times, qualifies her as a credible and professional mom.

As a mother of a special needs child, Nicole is also very experienced in recognizing developmental difficulties, and has spent seven years developing her skills as an advocate for her child. She has had hours of training and practice in specialized feeding therapy, as well as speech development and training for her special needs son. Her education in language teaching, and direct involvement in teaching kids a second language has allowed her to be proactive in helping develop the language skills of all her children.

She is currently working on other writing projects. Check out her website www.nicoleampi.com for updates on new titles and releases.

Although writing *cannot* and should not be her first priority, and it may take some time to complete her current projects, sharing her message is important to her. She will continue to write and will release additional titles as life allows.

Look For These Future Titles

Blindsided by Busy

Blindsided by Teens

Blindsided by Special Needs

Blindsided by Network Marketing

"Dinnertime Dictator"
by Michelle Sutherland BCBA

Made in the USA
Middletown, DE
12 March 2019